Take a Breath

The Path to Living Your Best Life

SHARON SIGURDSON DEUGO

Take a Breath

tellwell

Tellwell Talent
www.tellwell.ca

ISBN
978-0-2288-2758-0 (Hardcover)
978-0-2288-2757-3 (Paperback)
978-0-2288-2759-7 (eBook)

Disclaimer

This book is not intended to be a substitute for the services of health-care professionals. Neither the author nor publisher is responsible for any consequences incurred by those employing the processes outlined or reported in this book. Any application of the conditions outlined in the following pages is at the reader's discretion and is their sole responsibility.

Table of Contents

Chapter One

THE BEGINNING

My motivation for writing this book is simply to share what I have learned in the study of energy and consciousness. Working for the past 20 years researching, studying, training and building a practice to promote connection, healing and passion in my clients to live their best life has me living mine.

I graduated with a post-secondary bachelor of arts in psychology/sociology. I then worked for over 17 years in the field of human resource management in the public and private sector.

Due to a life-changing event in 2000, which I will detail in Chapter 2, I have spent the last 20 years studying, researching and training in a number of complementary therapies focusing predominately in the domain of consciousness and energy healing. I am currently taking time off from working as an energy practitioner, transformation life coach and mentor to write this book and enjoy my grandchildren, who are the greatest inspiration for taking on this project.

The most profound opportunities to learn come to us in the midst of turmoil and struggle.

The idea to write a book using the "breath" as a tool for transformation planted itself as a seed in my mind when I was struggling to find purpose, meaning and balance in my life. I have come to believe that some of the most profound opportunities to learn come to us in the midst of turmoil and struggle, and that is what happened to me.

I had somehow unplugged from the source of my joy in order to fill the needs and be present for everyone else in my life. I was giving all of my time and energy to raising a family, taking care of my home and supporting my husband as his career had him away more than he was home. Don't get me wrong—I completely understand that being selfless is not a bad thing. However, it can, and did, erode my sense of self. I was in my mid-thirties living a chaotic life when I had a "take a breath" moment.

Oprah Winfrey might call this type of experience an "aha" moment, for some it might be an awakening experience, maybe others "a dark night of the soul" and for me it was a "take a breath" and be present moment. I found myself in an *Eat, Pray, Love* (Gilbert, 2006) scene in my own bathroom, crying and releasing the most painful sadness in my heart. It actually took my breath away, and I cried until I had to take a breath or I would pass out.

Lying face up on the floor, looking at the ceiling, I allowed my breath to bring me back into my body and my pain. I remember saying out loud, "Why am I so unhappy?" With only the sound of my breath in my ears and the beating of my heart to keep me company, my mind cleared. In the silence and in the empty space between my breaths, I suddenly heard this quiet voice in my head, and it simply answered, "Because you are choosing to be."

What? I was stunned. Why would anyone choose to be unhappy? That was the craziest thought I had ever had. The power of that thought had me sitting up and then standing up. I felt angry at the voice and thought if that was God talking to me, it wasn't very helpful.

Just to put this moment in perspective, this was not the one that changed my life. However, it was the one that had me taking a deep breath to figure out the nature of my breakdown. The next few hours, days, weeks and months had me contemplating the idea that I was choosing to be unhappy.

I realized that my deep unhappiness was a sign for me to take inventory of my life and to fully realize that I had the power to change it. I honestly did not have a clue where I was supposed to start, but I knew if I did nothing my unhappiness was going to ruin me.

My despair on the bathroom floor was an act of surrender. I could no longer keep on going through the motions of living my life detached from the parts of me that made me feel like me.

That moment of authenticity created a breakthrough in my thought processes, and I was now paying attention to the things that I was doing that upset me and made me sad or unhappy. However, what truly made a difference for me was paying attention to the people, things and experiences that made me happy. The point to be taken here is that I was now paying attention to me, which was something I hadn't done in a very long time.

That voice in my head was guiding me to understand that being happy or unhappy was more about choosing consciously what I wanted to experience. I had spent so much time focusing on making other people happy that I had lost my own "happy." I realized that as I lost my happy, I was becoming bitter, resentful and negative in my own life. The filter of unhappy became the screen of my human drama.

The switch that flipped for me was a new understanding that if I was happy and focused on the things that mattered to me, I was actually a better person for the people in my life. This awareness created a power surge in me, and I had the clarity that the only happy I was responsible for was my own.

Now to some people, this might sound selfish, and I know that I was taught as a child that being selfish was a bad thing. I will talk about this "old" belief later in the book, but for now I actually had this unbelievable clarity that balancing selfless and selfish was possible and for the good of everyone in relationships.

Just to be sure you are following me, let me ask you, "Have you ever made someone else responsible for making you happy?" For example, have you ever said "if my spouse would just spend more time with me" or if they would do this or that then I would be happy? If my boss would just acknowledge how hard I work, I would be happy. If my kids would just sleep through the night or clean up their rooms, I would be happy. If only I lived in a bigger house, made more money or had a new car, I would be happy.

If you have had any thoughts similar to these, then you are—like I was—caught in the vortex of giving someone or something else your power to BE happy. Think about this for a moment. How you feel is personal. If you are unhappy and you feel it, you have the power to change it by doing something that can shift you into your happy. However, if you are unhappy because someone else won't do something the way you want them to, then your state of being is in their power to control, not yours.

How you feel is personal.

My intention is to demonstrate that if you are lost in the chaos of your busy life and busy mind, then you will most likely miss the opportunity to connect with the part of your "self" that may have gone missing because you weren't paying attention. Your story may be much like mine was. I lost my happy, but I was able to discover it again.

If you want to live your best life and you aren't quite there, it is possible to use your conscious breath when you find yourself in the midst of crisis, challenge, chaos, calamity and the craziness of life. You can change the experience to what you want versus what you don't want by bringing your consciousness to the party. In my example, the happy me is now my conscious choice and my conscious self. The part of me that is present and paying attention has taken over from the constant chatter in my mind that keeps me distracted and disconnected from what really matters.

I have set my personal goal and intention to shift my state of being from living in the past to staying present and fully conscious to what I am feeling so that I don't lose my happy. This may sound simple, and it is. However, it is not easy.

Shifting belief, perspective and mindset takes effort, commitment and daily practice. Much like an Olympic athlete who works towards the goal of a gold medal in their chosen sport, the repetition, practice and commitment to build the mental, physical and emotional muscles along with the neural pathways to create a champion are essential. Whatever goal you set for yourself, you have to have the will to make it happen through your daily work and practice.

Beginning with the end in mind means that you are now ready to set the intention to live your best life through your willingness to commit to the process. So, let's begin by doing just that.

THE HEART

The energy of the HEART is central to the message I am sharing with you. This cannot be overstated. When we separate from the energy of our hearts, we begin a journey away from our true nature, gifts, talents and purpose in life. A wounded and broken heart that is carried generationally through our family history, culture, religion and life leaves many of us discontent and disillusioned about life.

Living in the world today is not an easy task for any of us. The information overload, the busyness of day-to-day life and the demands of coping with the many challenges that cycle through our fields of influence leave many of us in the throes of overwhelm, anxiety, depression and sadness. It can happen with a simple word or situation that appears in our life. With the inability to regulate, calibrate and connect to the calming and loving energy of our hearts, we find ourselves in a daily struggle. The heart holds all of our secrets, all of our joy and our reason for being. It is only when you reconnect and put your "self" first that the heart can expand and grow to fill your life with all that you have been missing.

Take a Breath is my invitation to you to reconnect with your heart and all the parts of you that have fragmented over time. This book is meant to teach you how to bring your "self" into the moment and be present with the feelings that ignite gratitude, compassion and appreciation for all the good that exists in you and for you in the world.

When the heart opens, you will be connected to all the desires, hopes and dreams you once had and may have forgotten. The path you follow to reconnect with your heart is a personal and unique one. The heart connection offers you the chance to heal the past so that you can rediscover your purpose and passion in life. You are the only one who can decide if it is the path you want to take. Where hope exists, change is possible. BREATHE and ask your self "am I willing to open my heart to all the possibilities that exist for me to live my best life?"

"H.O.P.E. = HEARTS OPEN POSSIBILITIES ENTER" ~Sharon Deugo

THE BREATH

"Life is measured not by the breaths you take, but by the moments that take your breath away." ~ Corona/quoteinvestigator.com

This saying has always been a favourite of mine. At first, I interpreted it to mean that the moments that took my breath away were about the memories of the good times. They were the ones I thought I was supposed to remember as they measured how well I was living my life. More good memories represented a better life.

It wasn't until I started to work in the field of energy healing and transformation that I came to the realization that the moments that took my breath away were the ones that stopped me in my tracks and had me paying full attention to what I was experiencing. The beautiful sunsets, the sound of birds chirping, the cry of a child needing comfort, the loss of a loved one, the stillness in watching a deer walk past you in a forest, the horror of war and catastrophic events in the world—these are just a few examples of these moments. They happen when your senses are heightened and you are facing something that needs every ounce of your attention and intention to process in the moment.

> ***The moments that took my breath away were the ones that stopped me in my tracks and had me paying full attention to what I was experiencing.***

These moments have you present, alert and conscious of life happening, and it is in these moments that I have discovered the great mystery of life. The breaths we take, each one of them can be intentional and on purpose. Every time we take a conscious breath, we can be brought into the present moment and experience that one moment and then let it go so that it becomes part of the moments that take your breath away. I have so often thought of the time wasted being lost in thought and reliving moments from the past that had me miss the moment I was presently living. Have you ever said or heard someone else say in frustration or anger "I will never get this time back"?

Reimagining my life taking one breath at a time allows me to understand that I get to choose at any moment what I want to experience by simply giving myself permission to "take a breath." When I stay present and let whatever is happening move through me, it becomes a moment in my life to be experienced to the fullest, no matter the circumstances or situation. The release of the breath, coupled with the memory, leaves space for the next moment to appear and clear. Life happening expressed in terms of energy is simply to "let go and let flow."

> ***Life happening expressed in terms of energy is simply to "let go and let flow."***

When I began my own healing journey, I had difficulty remembering the memories of the good things in my life as I had held on too tightly to the painful ones. Those memories kept me stuck and numb in my life as I held my breath and clung to the past. But I learned to breathe again and to accept life happening. Courageously, I learned to let go of what no longer served me. These acts were the way back to living my best life. What I have learned is that letting go of the memories that have you holding your breath and living in the past is one of the clues to the mystery of discovering how to live your best life.

The stories, lessons and exercises in this book invite you to become a detective in your own life to uncover all the moments when you took a breath and forgot to exhale. The in-breath and out-breath is the mechanism that will change your life when you understand the principles of energy as they apply to the human experience. The beauty of this knowledge is that it doesn't cost a penny. This mechanism is perfectly designed so that everyone can connect to the breath to use it to manoeuve through the obstacles and pathways that appear in their life on a daily basis.

The content of this book will guide you through the data, information, knowledge and wisdom that I have gained in travelling down the path focused on the moments that take my breath away. I hope you enjoy the read and, in the process, discover something magical about yourself and the life you are intended to live.

THE PATH TO LIVING YOUR BEST LIFE

Genesis 2:7: "Then the LORD God formed man of dust from the ground, and breathed into his nostrils the breath of life; and man became a living being." ~ biblereference.com

Do you have any memories of someone saying to you "take a breath"?

I can. It is a memory of my mother's soothing voice and gentle manner while rocking me in her arms and coaching me to "take a breath." I was seven or eight years old and had just fallen out of a tree. She found me screaming and crying and unable to tell her what happened. I hurt everywhere and I was so scared. Her voice broke through the terror of my pain, and all I heard was "take a breath." With each breath, my body calmed, the crying diminished and the pain subsided. I was then able to tell her what had happened. She checked me over and nothing was broken. I only had a few bruises coupled with a new respect for heights. I remember I felt better and comforted with each breath I took.

> ***The sustaining mechanism of that life is our breath.***

Although I was not aware of it at the time, I do know now that the simple act of using my breath back then and now has the power to change a difficult situation into something less difficult. It may seem like a simple awareness to acknowledge; however, I do believe most of us take the ability to breathe for granted.

You have probably noticed that breathing is not something we have to think about because our bodies do it naturally. We don't have to think, blink or act—the breath of life just is. Science will tell you that our subconscious mind actually takes care of most of our physiological functions without a conscious thought on our part.

Take a moment to contemplate this amazing process. The gift of life itself is awesome. However, understanding that the sustaining mechanism of that life is our breath is highly significant. Naturally, knowing this on a conscious level makes our breath more interesting and certainly something that we can spend more time investigating.

This book, *Take a Breath: The Path to Living Your Best Life*, is about that investigation. My intention is to offer a perspective on the "conscious breath" to bring awareness to a process that was designed to bring ease and balance to our day-to-day life. Using the conscious breath as my tool of choice, I will guide you on a journey inward to the soul and the substance of your being.

The mechanism of the conscious breath is to create a pause in your thoughts as you focus your attention on the act of breathing. When we take our attention off our breath, our minds can run amok with the reel of life playing without interruption. More than likely you have experienced "monkey mind," when your thoughts take you into overwhelm and confusion as you try to work through your day-to-day life and challenges.

The conscious breath can be used as an instrument to bring healing to our hearts and minds especially at a time when many of us may feel like our spirit is broken and the call of our heart has been silenced.

It is my intention to demonstrate that the conscious breath can be used as an instrument to bring healing to our hearts and minds especially at a time when many of us may feel like our spirit is broken and the call of our heart has been silenced. This book is meant for anyone who feels they might be in a "difficult situation" and they want to make it "less difficult."

Stephen Covey, author of the book *The Seven Habits of Highly Effective People*, coined the phrase "begin with the end in mind." He wanted people to create a vision for their life and then live that vision through strategies that would guide them daily on the path to creating that vision. This book is in alignment with the principle captured in Stephen Covey's phrase "begin with the end in mind."

The following questions will help you determine if this is the book for you to begin the process of figuring out if you are living your best life.

Questions to ask yourself:

1. Am I living my best life? This would translate into you feeling happy and content in all spheres of your life: social, personal, health, education, religion, work/finances and spiritual.
2. Would you like to live your best life?
3. Would you be willing to look closely at your belief systems, patterns and habits of experience and behaviour that are sabotaging your ability to live your best life?
4. Are you ready to put time, effort, focus and commitment towards the work required to live your best life?
5. Are you open to new ideas, concepts and strategies that might contradict many things that you have been taught through the years? In other words, will you read and practise the new ideas, skills, principles and strategies with an open mind and most importantly an open heart?
6. Can you begin this journey by intentionally setting your goal to live your best life and believing it is possible?

If you have said "yes" to these questions, then it means you are ready to embark on a journey to discover all the parts of you that are ready and waiting for you to begin living your best life. If you said "no" to any of these questions, then this is not the book for you. However, if your curiosity gets the best of you, I would offer that it is a good read to get you thinking about life and wondering if there might be something you are missing. I always love a good mystery—how about you?

If you are ready, then let's begin. The only thing you have to remember is that the only obstacle in your way is you. Let's get to work and figure out how you can get out of your own way and start living your best life.

CREATING THE FIELD OF POSSIBILITIES

Setting an intention is simply offering your "goals" to the universe through whatever medium works for you. I like to write, so I wrote my intention to live my best life in my journal. You can paint it, sing it, share it with someone or use a vision board, among other creative ideas. However, the first requirement is to create the field for it to exist outside of your imagination.

I call this creating the field of possibilities. If you don't imagine something and then create that something through your thoughts, words, actions and effort, the question remains "can it or does it exist?" I liken this to the work of a designer. Everything that you can see in the world that was made by humans was first in the imagination of the person who designed it. For example, I have no idea who conceived the first idea of a chair; however, I have seen hundreds if not thousands of different chair styles and designs created for practicality, comfort and safety. Therefore, if the person who conceived of it didn't follow through, his or her "version" of that chair would never have existed.

> ***Setting an intention is simply offering your "goals" to the universe.***

This is true for all of us. If you want to live your best life, what are you putting out into your field to create the possibility of it happening? Let me give you an example.

I had put out into my field of possibilities the idea of writing a book. When my personal life coach, Derek Rydall, asked me in one of my sessions how my book was coming, I had a litany of excuses for why I had not started it. I said that I was so busy, I had family responsibilities, I had aging parents, and on and on. He said to me, "Sharon, I can tell you why you are not writing." I jumped to hear his brilliant assessment of my situation, and he simply said, "Your book is not coming along because you are choosing not to write. That is the only reason you are not writing—because you're not!"

What? It was another "take a breath" moment for me. Remember my "you are not happy because you are choosing not to be" moment? Well, here I was with the universe showing me again the same habit and pattern of behaviour in another area of my life.

This was no joke. I had been working for years on figuring out how to live my best life and here I was again using old habits to keep me stuck. This coaching was back in 2010, and trust me, I had been writing a lot. I started and stalled writing this book so many times with so many different titles and directions. What I discovered was that the book was in me, but I needed to do the work to let my message gain clarity in my own life and those that it would touch when it was finished. The work I have done in my practice during the last nine years is central to this book. Had I written the book before all that experience, it would have contained a totally different content and message.

This book will teach you things it took me years to grasp, practise and embody in my daily life. The process I teach stretches most people's belief systems beyond the possibilities that exist in their current lives. As I said earlier, if you are willing, this process will allow you to see where your imagination will take you if you are open and feeling adventurous. This is where my "inner detective" was ignited and got me moving towards the information I am now sharing with you.

Think of your vision as the seed of your potential.

To understand the concept of creating the field of possibilities, I want you to think of your vision as the seed of your potential. I will outline six essential conditions to identify the requirements for your seed to germinate, grow and sustain itself.

Derek Rydall, founder of the Law of Emergence and author of the book *Emergence*, used the analogy of an acorn to explain this concept. He said that the acorn is the seed of the mighty oak tree. Within the acorn is all the material that is required for it to grow into its glory. However, not every acorn makes it to its full potential. The reason is that each acorn did not receive all the conditions in nature necessary to survive and thrive. The seed requires fertile soil and enough rain, sun and space to grow. Without all the essential ingredients, the acorn will lay dormant until the right conditions are met.

Consider yourself a "seed" with unlimited potential to grow into the most magnificent vision that you have for yourself and for your life. Understanding and activating the following six conditions are essential for your seed to awaken to its potential.

Chapter Two

THE SEEDS OF YOUR POTENTIAL

Condition 1. CONSCIOUSNESS: the awareness or perception of something by a person (*Oxford Dictionary*)

The first condition in the process of living your best life is your CONSCIOUSNESS: whatever you consciously focus on can be created. However, if you store away your perceptions, dreams and aspirations, they will stay locked in a vault called your subconscious mind, where their manifestation will rely on direct action by you to bring them into your awareness in the present moment.

Whatever you consciously focus on can be created.

Think about the designer again. If a designer merely conceived of a chair in his mind without drawing it and then forming it into a workable model, there would be no chair, just the thought of one. The same would be true in the example I gave about finding "my happy." If I never had the perception or awareness that I was unhappy, I may never have been activated to figure out what my happy looked like.

Consciousness is present-moment awareness of what is happening in your life now. Take a breath, which is a direct action by you to stay present with me as I continue to explain the importance of your consciousness. In his book *The Power of Now*, Eckart Tolle writes about consciousness and the importance of the present moment to handle life challenges. He is a real pioneer in the study of consciousness and its effect on our health and life balance, so please put this book on your reading list to gain further insight into staying present.

The condition of consciousness might be easier to understand as it relates to learning a new skill. I will use the example of learning how to drive a car.

The process to obtain a driver's licence is a consciousness exercise as it requires you to pay full attention and often demands you take a driver's education course that will teach you how to drive via a step-by-step process. This requires your full attention.

If you can remember your driver's course, the in-class sessions were learning the rules of the road and about the vehicle you would be driving. Each part of the car was described, and you had to learn the function and purpose of each part as it relates to the whole vehicle. Once you became familiar and conscious of all the moving parts and rules of the road, the on-road driving sessions would begin. Every step was taught to ensure your safety along with the safety of the other drivers on the road. You had to study the information and to practise your skills repeatedly until driving became automatic.

Once you successfully completed the program, you were tested for on-road driving. If successful, you would receive your graduated driver's licence and could officially drive on your own. Again, this required repetition and practice until you mastered the use of the vehicle, including mirrors, signals, brakes and speed. Every step taken was conscious and deliberate.

The interesting thing that happens after you learn a new skill like driving is that over time all the rules that you had learned and had to systematically repeat each time you drove with your instructor soon became automatic. You would check your mirrors, turn your blinker on and stop at a red light, all the while talking on your phone or listening to the radio, without a conscious thought to take any of the actions required. This is called your subconscious mind.

The point to understand is that the conscious mind is present. It is aware of what is happening in the moment you are living and experiencing right now. It is awake and alert. When we are not present, we are often lost in thought, thinking about either the past or imagining something into the future. The importance of the conscious mind and our consciousness is that it gives us real-time information about what is happening now and is useful for decision-making and planning for what is necessary and important to do in our daily lives.

If you are unconscious, either literally or figuratively in terms of being lost in thought or unaware of your surroundings, the subconscious mind takes over and begins to run your day-to-day life using old habits and thought patterns to organize and run your life without any real input from your conscious mind. This might sound helpful; however, it is not. When you lose connection to the present moment through unconscious thought, feeling or action, you actually begin to miss the moments of your life because of the to-do lists in your head and the constant chatter of your busy mind that can cause overwhelm and chaos in your life.

The condition of consciousness is essential for you to be able to connect with the parts of you that are seeking to live your best life. If you stay stuck in the past or constantly plan for the future, how can you connect with what is important to do in the present so you can create your best life now and into the future? Do you remember the sunset I was talking about earlier? If you are lost in thought and distracted, that gorgeous setting sun might happen with you missing out on its beauty and wonder. I believe that we all could use more beauty and wonder in our lives, so maybe it's time to take notice, take a breath and stay present.

Condition 2. SUBCONSCIOUS MIND: the part of your mind that notices and remembers information when you are not actively trying to do so, and influences behaviour even though you do not realize it (*Cambridge Dictionary*)

Moving from conscious mind to SUBCONSCIOUS MIND is a process that has wonderful benefits, as well as some dire consequences if we don't pay attention and understand how it works.

The subconscious mind is incredible. It has the capacity to process billions of bits of information at once to sustain and maintain our physical bodies. Remember, we don't have to tell ourselves to breathe, our heart to beat, our digestive system to release enzymes to break down our food or our immune system to activate when we are faced with an illness. This ability is part of the human blueprint for survival.

The other aspect of the subconscious mind that must be considered is that it functions much like a supercomputer. It stores all the data, information and knowledge that we absorb through our senses. Whatever we see, feel, hear, touch, taste, smell or intuit is captured and stored on the hard drive of our subconscious mind. Each experience—and reaction to that experience—has a file created and it becomes a resource for the subconscious to access when making decisions on how to handle situations of a similar nature in the present.

The subconscious mind functions much like a supercomputer. It stores all the data, information and knowledge that we absorb through our senses.

Basically, the subconscious will reach into the recesses of your mind, pull out past data and use it in the present. Similar to the process of learning how to drive, this automatic response can be extremely beneficial when your reflexes are activated instantaneously when you have to react quickly to changes on the road. Muscle memory, coupled with the experience and practice of driving, created this reflex action that can serve us very well.

However, the downside of this process is that some of our past experiences may not be the most appropriate response to situations in the present. Psychological studies have shown that developmentally children's greatest learning phase in understanding the world they live in is during experiences that they had before the age of six or seven. This means that many people who are not living their best life are stuck in habits of thought and behaviours that developed as a result of the experiences that occurred when they were young and their minds were just developing.

Remember that each one of us was born into a family, culture, religion and community that provided the framework for our physical, mental, emotional and spiritual development. The uniqueness of our experience created how we perceive the world, and that perception became real to us as we grew into our adult life. If you have siblings and have had conversations about your childhood, rarely do any of you share the same experience.

I have three siblings, and when we had this discussion it was amazing how different each one of us viewed our "growing-up years." There are so many factors that can influence this, including gender, birth order and education. However, it does beg the question "what is really 'real'?"

If our subconscious mind can replay past events to overwrite present events based on a child's perception of what is real, is it really real? This question is definitely complicated. What I know to be true in my own experience is that I created certain beliefs about life when I was a child as a result of being influenced by parents, siblings and the world at large. However, through my own healing process, I have discovered that many of these beliefs are not real. They are simply a thought or a perception that I can change at any time.

Let me use an example. In my healing practice, I worked with a client who had long suffered with many setbacks in her life related to career and relationships. When we began working together, she had shared with me some of her experiences and asked me what I thought was happening that created these repeat experiences. First, I was grateful that she recognized that her experiences were repetitive. Second, I knew that she had a core belief about herself that was imbedded in her subconscious and it was recreating her experience by design.

Using the various tools I had acquired as an energy practitioner, we were able to uncover a deeply rooted belief she had about herself. This lovely lady was born into a family of six children and landed in the middle of the bunch. Her mother had been distant with her and would constantly remind her that she didn't quite measure up to her expectations.

The underlying belief that she was not good enough or worthy enough to have a loving relationship had her, now at age 60, living alone and at odds with what to do with the rest of her life. As we excavated the "unworthy" belief, she realized that she had made many decisions in her life on a subconscious level to not pursue a relationship or a career opportunity because the "program" of unworthiness was playing in the background of her mind.

She said she would often think, "Why bother staying in this relationship? He will probably leave me anyway." Or she would think, "It doesn't matter how hard I work; nothing every works out the way I want it to anyway." There was a part of her that believed that she wasn't worthy of the dreams she imagined. Remember, often our beliefs stem from our experiences as a child. Growing up in an environment where you are not celebrated and valued can leave an enduring wound, unless it is brought into consciousness when we are adults to question and change it.

"One of the pitfalls of childhood is that one doesn't have to understand something to feel it. By the time the mind is able to comprehend what has happened the wounds of the heart are already deep."
~ Carlos Ruiz Zafon in *The Shadow of the Wind*

The truth is if you choose—either consciously or unconsciously—to be a victim, you are basically giving away your power to be in charge of your life.

Before I move on, I want to share what I have come to know as a truth. You are only a victim of "your" life circumstances if you choose to be. It is a decision you make for yourself. The truth is if you choose—either consciously or unconsciously—to be a victim, you are basically giving away your power to be in charge of your life.

In the example above, my client who was mistreated by her mother had to learn to shift her perspective from blaming her mother for how she lived her life to taking responsibility for her life decisions. Again, I stress that this process sounds simple, and it is; however, it is not easy. It means that you have to shift a mindset or belief that has been engrained in you from past experiences.

There is an inherent sadness to the reality that many children grow up in environments where they are mistreated by their caregivers or in their community, culture or education. However, I have discovered both personally and professionally with many clients that there is this enduring quality within each of us that is striving to understand our purpose and reason for being.

When our subconscious beliefs sabotage our ability to connect with this inner guidance mechanism, we can lose our "self" to the thoughts and opinions of those who are influencers in our life. It is in adulthood that we have the opportunity to question our childhood experiences and dive deep to ask the questions about our life so that we can find the inner genius that will guide each of us to the truth of our true nature. Spoiler alert: that truth for each of us is that our true nature is LOVE. Yes, I said that four-letter word. Our inner guidance system is hard wired to be love. There will be more discussion on this later in the book.

> ***Our inner guidance system is hard wired to be love.***

This takes us to the next condition that you need to understand in order to live your best life. Understanding the human "energy" system is essential for you to grasp your potential. Take a breath, calm your busy mind, slow your heart rate and open your heart. You need to be conscious and present as we dive into this next section.

Did you take that breath? Are you ready to input some data and information that will create a knowledge base that will allow you to step into the wisdom of knowing yourself in a new way? If yes, let's get started … breathe.

> **Condition 3. ENERGY: the capacity or power to do work, such as the capacity to move an object (of a given mass) by the application of force. Energy can exist in a variety of forms, such as electrical, mechanical, chemical, thermal or nuclear, and can be transformed from one form to another. In physics and chemistry the Law of Conservation states that energy can neither be created nor destroyed, it can only be transformed or transferred from one form to another.** (*dictionary.com* and *thought.ca*)

The definition of ENERGY helped me put into perspective that everything that I can see, feel, touch, hear and sense in my surroundings is a form of energy. Like the definition says, energy exists in many forms and its nature is to move. Hence, energy that moves has the power to impact or change whatever it is moving towards. If energy isn't moving, it is stagnant, stuck, blocked, stalled or simply not working.

Let me offer an analogy to explain how the energy of the physical body works. I like to use the example of an architect who designs a beautiful building. She draws the blueprints and creates various rooms in the building that have specific uses and functions. Once the "floor plan" is laid out, the mechanical parts of the building are added, such as the electrical, plumbing, heating and cooling systems. Without the mechanical parts of the building, the building would not be livable or workable.

> ***Energy exists in many forms and its nature is to move.***

The physical body can be viewed in much the same way. If you think of the design or blueprint of the physical body, you can consider each part as a room with a specific use or function. If you think of each body system, all the organs, glands and tissues within that system have a job to do. For example, the circulatory, respiratory, digestive, muscular, immune, reproductive and elimination systems are required in order for the body to be livable. These are the rooms, and now the "mechanical" parts of the human body/building need to be added.

If you are following me, you will realize that the animating force of the physical body is our "life force energy." Our life force energy begins within the womb of our mother. Our mother's "energy system" begins the process of incubating a new life within her. Once birthed, the child begins life separate from the mother when it takes its first breath.

Do you now see the connection to the importance of the breath? Your breath is energy moving into and out of your body. If your breath is moving and you are conscious of it, then you will be able to manage the moment you are currently experiencing with greater balance and clarity. When subconscious, the breath sustains life, but when brought into consciousness, the breath has the double duty of bringing balance and clarity to the present moment. This awareness has the potential to demonstrate how capable and powerful our "life force energy," also referred to as the "human spirit," has been designed.

Without energy moving in, through and out of our bodies, we would not be alive. Here's the nugget. If everything in the universe is some form of energy, then as a human being how do I connect with my life force energy to ensure that my physical body is in balance and in harmony with living my best life?

It wasn't until the year 2000 that this question became important to me. My interest in the human spirit (or life force energy) was activated when my husband was admitted to a critical care unit of a hospital. His illness had been difficult to diagnose and within a time frame that made the doctors uncertain whether he would survive. When the doctors finally determined he had contracted cryptococcal meningitis, it was literally the eleventh hour for my husband, leaving our family terrified of the outcome.

The animating force of the physical body is our "life force energy".

There was a moment in the hospital when I was alone with my husband. For several hours, we had been in the intensive care unit while the medical staff ran tests to find answers to this illness that was raging through my husband's body. As I sat with him, all the sounds and smells of the hospital wrapped around me. I had this sudden awareness that this was a moment of truth, a moment of surrender. There was absolutely nothing that I could do to assist my husband, and it was now up to whatever forces existed in and around him that would determine his survival.

I remember bowing my head in prayer, although I am not religious. It was not my practice to pray. However, I had a deep belief in "something" greater than myself that somehow worked as a guiding force in my life. I have since come to realize that this belief is my definition of spirituality. (I will discuss this topic in greater detail later in the book.) Because of this personal relationship I had with this "something," I reached deeply in prayer to connect in this moment. I spoke openly about my life and my heart's desire to surrender to whatever was to happen for my husband. I offered that I was willing to release control and allow my husband to follow his path. I remember thinking that I would survive whether he lived or died. I simply didn't want my husband to suffer in a manner that would diminish his will to live a full and wonderful life.

I prayed. I wept. In surrender, I held my husband's hand and clung to the hope that he would return to me. It was in this state that my attention was drawn to the energy I felt in the room. I looked up to see if someone had entered, and then for the briefest of seconds there was a stillness I cannot explain. Then there was a gust of air moving through the room, and the curtains surrounding all the beds billowed at once and a light brighter than I could have imagined appeared and then it was gone. The next moment, my husband, who had been unconscious, squeezed my hand. As I turned to look at him, he had a smile on his face and he simply said, "Hey, Shar, I am not going anywhere."

That moment changed my life, as it became the catalyst that propelled me into the study of energy, healing, human consciousness and the human spirit. My husband's stay in the hospital was a demonstration of what the human energy system or spirit can do when focused on outcome. Doctors repeatedly gave my husband time frames of recovery and healing. In every instant, he would respond with his own vision of how he saw his recovery. The doctors would say that it would take two months to get to this level. My husband would say, "No, I will be out of here in two weeks." And he was.

My husband had the medical staff stumped on how it was possible. Every time he would set a goal and stayed focused on the outcome he wanted, he succeeded. It was amazing to watch. Once we were home and the healing continued, I was able to begin my journey of trying to understand what I had witnessed and experienced in the hospital.

This life-changing event caused my life to take on a whole new trajectory, and I found myself entering a new field of discovery. The seed had been planted, and my curiosity became the fertilizer to pursue the study of the human energy system.

Learning about energy was absolutely the most interesting and amazing time of my research phase. I didn't even know where to start so I focused my attention on the experience I had in the hospital when I had surrendered to my husband's condition and let go of outcome.

I remember feeling something amazing in that moment of stillness. It was a freedom like I had never felt. It felt like the burden of everything I was carrying was lifted and I was being cradled in the arms of a loving parent who would take care of everything. The feeling was bliss. I wonder if this is how a newborn baby must feel in the arms of a loving parent—warm and secure.

The first task for me was to find the answer to what connected me to that "feeling" of bliss. Second, my desire was to learn how to experience it more deeply and definitely more often in my life.

This led me to work with a spiritual counsellor/teacher/mentor, Kristina Jansz, for a period of well over four years. In the process of learning about spirituality and connecting with something greater than myself, I realized that "energy" was about focusing attention on what it was I wanted to experience versus what I didn't want. Kristina Jansz was the first to say to me, "Sharon, what you focus your attention on will become your reality." She taught me to go inward to understand my own energy input and output to determine what was holding me back and what was moving me forward in my life. In other words, I had to begin to understand myself before I could understand the bigger picture of how I was creating my life experience.

I realized that "energy" was about focusing attention on what it was I wanted to experience versus what I didn't want.

"What you focus your attention on, will become your reality."
~ Kristina Jansz

The sentence above can be life changing if you pay attention to the definition of energy. Remember, energy has the capacity to move an object and it can come in many forms. Therefore, if you take the statement above as a truth, you will accept the fact that the energy it takes to focus on something means that what you think, speak, believe, feel and sense about your life will create how you experience your life. This means that thoughts, words, actions, feelings and beliefs are energy and they are creative by nature. These are the human "energy" currencies that make up our "life force energy" to create the life of our dreams.

"Your beliefs become your thoughts,
Your thoughts become your words,
Your words become your actions,
Your actions become your habits,
Your habits become your values,
Your values become your destiny."
~ Mahatma Gandhi, Indian political and spiritual leader (1869–1948)

Accepting that our life force energy or spirit is composed of what you think, say, do, feel and believe—and how you express them in your life—is critically important. Referring back to Condition 1, consciousness, and Condition 2, subconscious mind, you must be aware that your life force energy or spirit—whether conscious or subconscious—is causal in how you experience life. Thus, if you are not paying close attention (consciously aware) to what you are thinking, saying, doing, believing and feeling, you may be creating or causing experiences or situations in your life that you do not want.

Moreover, if you are suppressing your life force energy in your thoughts, words, actions, feelings and beliefs, then you are creating stagnation, blockage, constriction or restriction in your life experience. Remember the architect who designed the beautiful building? Imagine what happens when the plumbing becomes clogged or there is a short circuit in the electrical system and the lighting doesn't work. The building owner has to ensure that all systems are running smoothly and that the energy is flowing for the safety, security and health of all those living in the building. Think about what might be occurring in your physical body if your life force energy is not moving in, through and out of all of your body systems to maintain and sustain health. More will be discussed on the physical body later in the book.

Remember my client who had difficulty with her relationships and career? What we discovered is one of her core beliefs growing up was that she was unworthy of living her best life based on what she perceived her mother had taught her. This belief blocked her life force energy from imaging her life to be what she had originally dreamed. She was able to remember defining moments throughout her life when her thoughts, words, actions and feelings were in alignment with this belief, creating exactly what she believed to be true, which was that she was unworthy of love and success in her life. As we worked on strategies to create a new belief in her conscious mind that she was indeed worthy of all the best that life and love could offer, her experiences began to shift.

In my husband's healing journey in the hospital, I can see an alignment between his focused intention to recovery and what he believed, said, did, felt and thought in order to recover. His life force energy had been activated and aligned to heal. There is no disputing that the medical care, drug intervention and support systems surrounding him were a huge part of the healing process. However, his focus and intention were directed toward what he wanted to experience, and in the end we were able to celebrate his return to health and balance. I know that this is not the outcome for everyone who is diagnosed with a life-threatening illness. However, my husband's story offers a perspective on the healing process and the importance of our conscious attention to support what we want to experience.

> ***The space that surrounds you is considered a "field of energy,".***

Take a breath. Clear your mind and contemplate this last paragraph. Ask yourself this question: "Is it possible that who I am and what I accomplish in my life is based on what I believe, think, feel, act and say about myself?" If the answer to this question is "yes, it is possible," then you must see how important it is to take stock of where you are right now in your life and determine if the beliefs, thoughts, feelings, words and actions are aligned with living your best life.

This information is exciting to contemplate and even more exciting when you begin to apply it to your daily life. However, there is another aspect of energy that is essential for you to understand in order for you to have a complete picture of how energy will guide you into living your best life. The energy that you project through your life force energy will impact the energy that surrounds you. Although the space between us appears to be empty, it is not. The space that surrounds you is considered a "field of energy," and it will be impacted by the energy you project from your physical body through the energy currencies I have identified.

Let me briefly explain what I mean when I use the term field of energy. The energy that moves through your physical body is called your life force energy. Your life force energy is what animates the physical body and creates communication networks between all your body systems to sustain and maintain balance in the body. The energy that moves through your body is connected to the energy that surrounds your body. The energy that surrounds your body is the "field of energy" that you are connected to.

An excellent resource to understand this at a deeper level is Donna Eden's book, *Energy Medicine.* I also recommend Lynn McTaggert's book, *The Field.* Both authors explain in depth that the "field of energy" around you connects you to the "collective" and will determine how you experience energy. It is also important to understand that everyone's field of energy is unique to them and will impact "the field" based on their projections determined by their life experiences and belief systems.

What became extremely fascinating for me was the discovery of how the life force energy of all living organisms can be accessed and impacted through hands-on healing techniques to create movement, balance and connection. The next condition outlined will help to explain how we can better manage our life experiences through understanding the laws of energy as they relate to the concept of intention.

Remember, at the beginning of this book I said the intention of the book was to assist people who are in a difficult situation to learn to use their breath to shift them into a less difficult situation. The next condition becomes essential to awaken you to the potential that lies within you to live your best life.

Condition 4. INTENTION: an intention is an idea that you plan (or intend) to carry out. If you mean something, it's an intention. Your goal, purpose, or aim is your intention. It's something you mean to do, whether you pull it off or not. (*vocabulary.com*)

Being aware that an INTENTION is energy is an important condition to understand and embrace. Remember the discussion earlier about "what you focus your attention on will become your reality." This is basically the outcome of an intention. The energy of an intention is activated by our mind, whether it is conscious or subconscious.

I studied various healing and energy modalities that offer hands-on healing, including reflexology, reiki and therapeutic touch. They all use "energy" as a term to describe how you approach a client to do healing work. When you set the "intention" to do a healing session, you are actually establishing a connection with the client to work in their field of energy without disrupting your own.

The intention and goal of an energy practitioner is to move energy in their client's field and physical body to promote healing, relaxation and balance. The practitioner understands that energy follows the intention of the person who sets it. Energy will follow intention, whether it is conscious or subconscious. The concern here is that if you are sending unconscious intentions out into your field of energy, then you will in all likelihood create an experience you don't even realize that you had initiated or even wanted.

Remember that life force energy is made up of your beliefs, thoughts, words, actions and feelings. When you consciously or unconsciously send out loving thoughts to someone, even though the words are not said, a person can pick up or sense what you are sending. The same is true when you send out thoughts of negativity towards a person. Remember the law that energy once created cannot be destroyed. Energy is energy, so whether you want to accept it or not, the truth is that all of your energy, when moving or not, consciously or unconsciously, will become creative or stagnant depending on your intention.

A "thought" is energy and it will travel from your field of energy to the energy in the field that surrounds you. It is like a vibration or frequency that will travel outward until it connects or attracts itself to that which it is like. In science, this is called radiation and magnetization. This simply means that whatever energy (beliefs, thoughts, words, feeling and actions) you radiate, you will magnetize back as an experience and vice versa. This idea might be easier to understand if I use an analogy.

When plugged in and turned on, a radio can be set at a specific station and then you can listen to your favorite DJ and music. The frequency of energy for each radio station has a name, and you simply have to turn that dial to the call letters and name of the radio station, and like magic you are connected. Now of course, it isn't magic, because there are satellites and radio towers that allow this process to work.

Your life force energy and its frequencies are much the same as a radio. Similar to a radio station, every person has his or her own unique name and energy signal or frequency. The unique frequency a person sends in the form of their beliefs, thoughts, words, actions and feelings will seek to find frequencies of a similar nature to connect with. You may have heard of the collective consciousness. If not, it is simply the empty space that appears around and between objects. The space is not empty, as I mentioned earlier. It is actually filled with the frequencies of energy being sent out from everyone and everything, everywhere; hence, it is called the collective and it contains the frequencies from the human and animal world. Therefore, anything, anywhere, affects everything, everywhere.

Let me share a personal story of how this works. I was at home dealing with a stressful situation concerning a family member who had just experienced a traumatic event. It was something that I had no control over, and I was feeling scared and vulnerable because there was nothing I could do to make it better. I felt my heart rate increase and my breathing became shallow. I remember beginning to cry when all of sudden the phone began to ring. When I picked it up, it was a dear friend. She apologized for calling "out of the blue" but she had been thinking about me when she picked up a very strong energy that something was wrong. She wanted to know if I was alright. Of course, I wasn't, and I was able to share with her my distress. She calmly talked me through it, and I felt my energy shift into a calmer and more relaxed feeling as I was better able to process what I was experiencing.

The important concept here is that my friend had connected with me through her conscious thoughts. Her energy frequency picked up mine through her intention when she was thinking about me, and she acted on her instinct to reach out. This story illustrates perfectly the conditions of conscious awareness and intention being activated through the energy connections between two people. My friend is an extremely intuitive person, and she focuses on that skill to guide her in her daily life. She taught me so much about staying present and connected to the energy that moves in, through and around me.

The lesson in this example is the understanding that gut instincts are messages from the physical body. If we are conscious and paying attention, these messages can be huge cues to making decisions in your daily life. I don't know if you have ever experienced a similar situation when you just sensed something wasn't right and you reached out to someone or someone reached out to you. This is a perfect example of how energy moves when we pay attention and connect with the frequencies that surround us.

The energy or thought seeks what is like it, meaning that it will connect with similar thoughts in the collective consciousness and will return back in the form of an experience, often magnified due to the energy it picks up on its return to you. This is much like your favourite music being played, and all of a sudden the volume goes up as everyone around is tuned into the same station at the same time.

> ***The Law of the Circle states that whatever energy you put out into the universe will come back to you full circle.***

The concept I have just explained is actually a scientific law of cause and effect. Some may call it the Law of Attraction. However, I prefer how author Patricia Cota Robles explains it in her books as the Law of the Circle. Basically, she explains that the law states that whatever energy you put out into the universe will come back to you full circle. She goes into great detail about how this energy works and uses examples from science (cause and effect, radiation, magnetization), religion (eye for an eye, tooth for a tooth; cast your bread upon the water) and spirituality (in-breath and out-breath). It's a truth that is sometimes difficult to grasp so I will clarify with examples from a couple of my client cases.

To preserve my client's confidentiality, I will call her Jane. She is a 45-year-old woman who was struggling with many issues in her life related to her health, career and, most particularly, her relationship with her husband.

When she came to me, she had been struggling for over 10 years to build her career, which she said was stalled. After 16 years of marriage, she was also in a phase where she and her husband were on the verge of separation as there was no communication or intimacy left.

Together, we identified some strategies that she agreed to work on to see if it would help to improve her life in a positive and pleasant way. Jane was excited to incorporate these strategies into her life. With conviction and commitment, she stuck to the plan and worked daily to improve her situation.

Following her fourth session with me, she reported that her career was taking off as her clients were lining up for her services. She further reported that her health challenges were also improving as her digestive issues had begun to regulate and she had more energy to plan daily workouts and focus on her diet.

However, the one area that seemed to get worse was the relationship with her husband. She shared how she had made all these amazing improvements in herself and was being more open, but her husband was always picking fights with her, finding fault and treating her disrespectfully. She blamed him for all that was wrong in their relationship.

As I listened to her describe her husband's behaviour, I waited for a pause and then asked her this question: "When your husband walks into a room where you are sitting, what is your immediate **thought** about him?" Without hesitation, Jane responded, "I am usually so irritated with him that I think pretty unpleasant things about him."

I said, "Okay. Now could you share with me how you **feel** about him when he walks in the room?" Jane looked at me and said, "Well, I usually am not very happy about his presence. He irritates me, and I find myself feeling so angry at him."

I said, "Okay, now that you know what you think and feel when he walks in the room, what is your **belief** about him when you are together?" Jane looked at me with tears in her eyes and she said, "I have this belief that things won't get better and I will never be happy."

My next question was this: " Okay, Jane, if you are now aware of how you think, feel and believe things about him, how and why would you expect your relationship with him to improve?" Jane was confused and said she didn't know how to respond to the question.

My response was to ask her if she thought it was possible that her husband was picking up her energy and was responding to her in the way she expected him to. Jane acknowledged that she could see that his behaviour might be in response to the way she was treating him and that there definitely seemed to be a connection. She realized that the way he was treating her was a mirror image of her own behaviour towards him. This became a huge "take a breath" moment for Jane.

I took this opportunity to share with her the "laws of energy" and how they worked through intention, both consciously and unconsciously. I explained to her that if she wanted to change her relationship with her husband, she first had to consciously decide (that is, set an intention or goal) what it was she wanted to receive from him in their relationship. If she wanted love and kindness, then she would have to mirror that behaviour in all of her thoughts, words, feelings, beliefs and actions towards her husband. It is like when you look in a mirror, you can't change the appearance of the reflection until you change the appearance of what is being reflected.

This became a turning point and an opportunity for Jane. If she changed her pattern of behaviour through intention by using her thoughts, feelings, words, actions and beliefs to better reflect what she wanted to experience, would it change her relationship with her husband?

Jane realized the situation was not about placing blame anymore, it was about accepting her part in making a change that would make her happier. Understanding that she was part of the problem, she was able to take responsibility for her energy and decide consciously with intention to be more supportive and loving towards her husband.

Together, Jane and I worked on some new patterns of thoughts she could use and practise when she and her husband were together. She agreed to practise them for a few weeks and to let me know how she was doing.

After sticking to the plan for several more weeks, she finally emailed me with some happy results. Here are a few quotes from her email:

> *"It's actually a very loving and happy environment in my house these days. My husband is jovial, playful, loving ... actually more affectionate than I think I can handle! ... Fewer harsh words and definitely more hugs."*

This example was a huge validation of how the Law of the Circle works and that intention is key in creating what we experience in life. When my client set the intention to focus on improving her relationship with her husband by taking responsibility for her energy, she was able to prevent conflict from arising. I guided my client to "take a breath," which is a conscious act to create a pause before she responded to her husband. Her intention was to shift her energy, whether in thought, feeling, word, action or belief, to give her the power to stay present and focus on what she wanted to receive back from her husband. She had to pause long enough to notice her husband's energy and try to shift it with her own.

> ***If anger meets anger in a relationship, the outcome is always conflict. If, however, anger is met with understanding, compassion and patience, conflict can be diverted.***

The truth is that if anger meets anger in a relationship, the outcome is always conflict. If, however, anger is met with understanding, compassion and patience, conflict can be diverted. The simple practice is to "take a breath" to give yourself time to clear your mind and connect with your heart. By practising with this tool, you will be able to make a more conscious decision about how to handle a situation in a more supportive and kind way.

Another example of using consciousness (or breath), intention and energy to shift behaviour happened with another client. This client was struggling with her relationship as well. She said that she and her partner were always arguing and that her nature was always to fight back and not to give in. Her partner's pattern of behaviour was to walk away or flee from the conflict. I asked her to think about the dynamics of this play that the two of them were acting out together, or as Dr. Phil would ask, "How is that working for you?"

I pointed out to her that energy follows a path. What we fight we fuel, and what we flee from will follow us. If she and her partner were setting up this pattern, it was no wonder they were repeating the same issues and difficulties in their relationship. The only way to change the situation was for one or both of them to take responsibility for their own habit or pattern of behaviour. The fact that she was consciously aware that she was "a fighter" gave her the opportunity to shift into a different behaviour if she wanted to improve her relationship.

Her subconscious programming over most of her adult years had created an incredibly competent, independent and successful woman. However, in relationships, this strong, powerful woman had forgotten how to trust and be vulnerable. The ability to consciously notice the pattern and then to set an intention, through this self-awareness, to shift into a gentler and compassionate energy created a different experience for her.

The "intention" of these examples is to provide a framework for you to see how important it is for you to take ownership of your own energy patterns and habits of behaviour. It is one of the hardest things to do. Most of us have been taught to feel like we are victims of circumstance and have no control of how life will unfold. I am convinced this belief is common among most of us.

The reason I mention this is because most young children feel they have little control of their environment and can hardly wait to be out on their own. I know as I grew into my teen years, I often thought about how great it would be to be out of my parents' influence so I could make my own decisions.

Little did I know that as an adult I would hold on to some of these old beliefs subconsciously only to discover in my own healing process that I often played the victim in my life story. Remember me giving away my "happy"? I believed that my job was to take care of others at the expense of my own well-being. I now understand that I was taught this through the generational belief of a woman's role in our culture. The role of the feminine, mother, caregiver and nurturer was all about being selfless and almost subservient to our masculine counterparts.

By taking on the victim role, I was able to more easily blame and project what was happening in my life onto someone else. If I wasn't happy, it had to be someone else's fault. As a victim, you will often feel unappreciated, unsupported, helpless and hopeless in life because you believe someone else is controlling your life and you have to follow the rules. When I was growing up, my father would often say to me, "While you live under my roof, you will live by my rules." This statement eventually formulated a belief that rules were put in place by people in positions of power and authority. If these rules were not followed, then there would be consequences. Even if I didn't always agree with my father's rules, I was more afraid of what would happen if I didn't follow them. I carried this "fear" into my adult life and would avoid conflicts by being the "good girl" and staying silent and invisible.

Once the victim appeared as a repeat pattern in my life drama, I quickly began to excavate the beliefs behind it. That is, I began to take ownership of this pattern and had to figure out what I believed that was causing me to feel unappreciated, unsupported, unlovable and invisible. The first step was for me to change my old pattern of belief and intentionally replace it with a new one in order to shift my experience.

I "intentionally" developed a belief statement that would support my shift in thought and behaviour. I consciously worked with it daily until it became an automatic response to life challenges. It went like this: **"I am not a victim of circumstance. I am powerful beyond my own knowing. I am in charge of my own life."** This became my new mantra or anthem, and I repeated it in my mind and took it into my heart every chance I felt or saw my victimhood show up.

Please take a moment right now to take these words into your heart. Take a breath, hold the space and let these words flow through you. Say them out loud. **"I am more powerful than my own knowing and I am in charge of my own life."** Feel the power and energy move through your body as you take ownership of the possibility that this belief is truth. Notice if your energy or mood shifts when you repeat these words. Energy comes in many forms. If these words make you feel better than before you said them, it means your energy has shifted and you are the one responsible for making it happen through your conscious attempt to change a habit or belief. This puts you behind the wheel and in charge of your human vehicle. How exciting is that!

You have probably heard the saying "fake it until you make it." The story I shared with you about believing I was a victim and then changing that belief is an example of this phrase in action. It is difficult to believe something when you are in the depths of despair and you feel beaten down by life. However, if you can just take a moment, take a breath, pause and with intention turn your mind off to allow the energy of your heart to open to the possibilities that are waiting for you to show up, then and only then will you be able to activate or shift into an energy that feels better. Sometimes merely saying what you want out loud with conviction, effort, commitment and passion—whether you believe it yet or not—will get you moving to where you want to be.

I prefer the phrase "fake it until you become it." Remember when I lost my happy? Well, I certainly had to fake it for a period of time before I actually believed it. The work I did to figure out what would make me happy had me moving into the field of happy over time, and with practice, patience and perseverance I was finally that … happy.

Please understand that happy as well as every other emotion is a state of being and it is always in you. It is up to you to bring that emotion or state of being into consciousness and be "it" no matter what is happening in your life. Challenges can knock you off balance. However, your capacity to move through the challenge is what can allow your energy to return to the state of being that you decide or choose consciously to be. This is a powerful awareness, so please pay attention and become the person you know you can be.

If you are waiting for someone or something to make you feel the way you want to feel, that is where you will stay, waiting. Stop waiting and just "act as if." Whatever you are seeking you already have within you. All you have to do is believe in your "self" and know you are in charge of your life when you are conscious and aware of what it is you want. Do you want to be happy? Then choose happy and become it.

Setting the intention to become the person you want to be is taking responsibility for your "self" and the energy you put out into your field of influence. Your energy will follow that intention, so be proactive and engaged with all the people and situations you most want to experience.

The alternative is to lose focus, connection and desire to follow the dreams you hold in your heart. The disconnection to your "self" is when your life will go off the rails and you will lose sight of what is important to you. Intention puts you in charge of "you" and your life, so take a breath and let's move on to the next condition that will support you living your best life. And guess what? The next condition is all about you and only you.

Condition 5. SELF: a person's essential being that distinguishes them from others, especially considered as the object of introspection or reflexive action (*Oxford Dictionary*)

The SELF is you. The key to living your best life is "knowing thyself," a.k.a. you. Here you are learning about the breath, consciousness, your subconscious, energy and intention, and now you have to apply all these conditions for the potential in you, self, to manifest so you are able to live your best life. I hope you are seeing the interconnectedness of all this information.

You are a unique expression of one life on a planet of billions.

Take a breath. Stay with me and reflect on the definition of self. "Self" in the definition is called your essential being. It states that you are a unique expression of one life on a planet of billions. Okay, I may have filled in a bit here, but the point is there is no one else like you on the planet. If self is about "being," then what are you "being" in order to live your best life?

Remember the acorn. It's just an acorn until the natural flow of the energy in nature has it buried by a squirrel in rich fertile soil, where the seed cracks open and its potential is nourished and it grows into a mighty oak.

Like the acorn, your potential exists within you as well. It is waiting for the right conditions to awaken through your human energy system and flow. Untapped potential is simply energy that is dormant due to the absence of the right conditions. Until you tap into your potential through conscious awareness, intention and single-minded focus on self, you will stay stuck and stalled right where you are.

Take a moment right now and think about a memory or time in your life when you took a risk and tried something you have never tried before and discovered that you were great at it. Through this process, you discovered some of your untapped potential waiting for you to nurture and grow within you.

This happened to me over 20 years ago. I found myself reflecting on a thought and belief about myself that I knew I had to test. The belief was that "I didn't have a creative bone in my body."

When I reflect on this belief now, I know that it was a self-limiting thought that was keeping me stuck at that time. Fortunately for me, my curiosity back then got the best of me, and I began to challenge this belief about myself. As the universe would have it, I happened to be in a friend's shop, and she had posters up on her wall advertising a decorative painting class for beginners. I couldn't even draw stick people well, but I wanted to see if I could learn and maybe tap into some of my "creativity."

Creativity is a natural impulse within all of us.

I signed up for the class, and over a two-year period I trained and was certified to become a decorative painting teacher. I worked in a local studio part-time to complete my experiment into the creative aspect of my potential. I was definitely not the best painter, but I was a great student and an even better teacher once I learned the basic skills and shared my knowledge with others.

It was an amazing experience, and what I discovered about myself was a "take a breath" moment. Whatever limits I put on myself was a choice. Creativity is a natural impulse within all of us, whether we create life through the birth of a child or we create through music, art, sport, teaching, medicine or any number of ways. It is your nature to create, and for you to believe anything different than this truth will only limit your potential and delay you in connecting with your passion and purpose in your life.

Decorative painting was a wonderful experience, but it was not my passion and was not my genius. What I discovered was that the process of learning and then teaching what I have learned absolutely resonated with me. I can feel myself getting excited whenever a new book, course, workshop or training opportunity shows up in my areas of interest. I will devour the contents and then apply what I have learned to the skill set I am building. Having this awareness about myself keeps me in the flow of my passion and purpose, and for all intents and purposes, it is guiding me to live my best life.

To know yourself is to connect with the parts of you that make you unique and special. Ask yourself, "What are my special talents, gifts, ideas, imagination, dreams, contributions, passions and abilities?" This is the first step in moving you in the direction of knowing who and what you are all about. Answering this question will empower you to crack open your seed of potential, to germinate and grow into what gives you purpose and passion in your life. You aren't alive today just to breathe air! You must have a passion, desire or impulse of some type that gets you up in the morning and gets you moving towards whatever your goals may be.

Everything that you need is already in the "blueprint" of your human energy system.

If you are stuck at this point because you have lost touch with yourself, then this part of the book may be just what the doctor ordered. In my practice, when I asked many of my clients what they wanted out of life, they would look at me with a blank stare or admit they had no idea. They would ask me to tell them what I thought they should do or be and to give them the secret to the universe. With every coach I worked with, I asked them to do the same for me. What I learned for myself and what I now share with my clients is that they are the only ones that possess the answers.

Everything that you need is already in the "blueprint" of your human energy system. The work that is needed is for you to focus your attention on the process of reconnecting to the dreams and passions that you had as a child. Remember, this connection is to the heart.

There are three conditions that I teach my clients to focus on as they relate to the "self." The first is awareness or consciousness as it relates to self. The second is care, and the third is love, again as it relates to self. The three are interconnected and are in no particular order of importance. However, they are necessary to understand if you want to live your best life. Self-awareness knows what you want in life and has you moving toward it. Self-care is putting your needs first, and by doing so, you are connecting to yourself through acts of love and attention, which translates to self-love. All of which most of us need more of.

The common theme in the majority of my clients is a disconnection from "self." This disconnection has caused them to create an idea or a persona of who they think they should be based on what they believe to be true. The persona is often called our ego, and it plays a role in presenting to the world a masked version of our true self. Many of us will not reveal our vulnerability, dark shadowy side or flaws to the world, because most of us fear a loss of "something" if people really know who we are without the mask.

The self is not an idea. It is real and it is you. However, a common malady of the human race is that we are born into a world already framed with the boundaries of what is possible within the family, country, culture, religion, educational institutions or government that we are born into. Most of us were taught to toe the line and follow the rules and patterns of the past generations.

> ***The power of who I am lies in what I believe about the world I live in.***

When we separate from our essential being, also known as our authenticity, we are diverted from the power that exists within our human energy systems and unconsciously connect to the belief systems and values that are outside of our self. As children, this is precisely what we do. We believe our parents, caregivers, educators, government and others without question.

We should not judge this as a bad thing. But each of us must realize that the power of who I am lies in what I believe about the world I live in. If you were taught lack and limitation is the truth, that it's a dog-eat-dog world, competition over collaboration and community, that there isn't enough, or I am not enough in the world, then your experience in life will reflect that based on the laws of energy. One of the most crippling beliefs that will keep you stuck and disillusioned about life is the belief that you are a victim of circumstance and have no control of what you experience. These beliefs can lead to your essential being losing its connection to the unique gifts, talents and passions you have as they are overridden by the collective belief systems of previous generations.

What I am offering to you in this section is for you to be willing to open your mind and heart to a different possibility that can lead you to living your best life by tapping into the potential of your essential "being." This is where you "take a breath," pause, clear your mind and join me on the journey to discover your "self" and connect with your passion and purpose in life. This becomes an inside-out job versus an outside-in job. This is exciting and terrifying all at the same time. However, if you are willing and committed to do the work, the results will be worth the risk you take in stepping into a new way of thinking and being.

Remember the acorn analogy. The acorn is probably content to stay an acorn and is happy to hang around on the tree or nestle into the grass until some squirrel finds it and buries it for winter food. Only a few of the acorns are fortunate enough to crack the seed so that the potential buried within their shells is released to germinate, grow and become a mighty oak. My question to you is this: "Are you ready to be the acorn that grows into a mighty oak?"

> ***When you are consciously aware of your breath, you are actually feeling the human energy system shifting in your body, and you are controlling it.***

SELF-AWARENESS

Take a couple of breaths for me. Draw your breath deeply into your lungs and pull it into your belly, if you can. Then slowly breathe it out. Do this several times, and then with the last breath I want you to imagine breathing directly into your heart, rather than into your lungs and belly. Place your hand over your heart if that will help. As you do this, I want you to keep breathing and imagine for a moment the power of the organ in your chest. The heart pumps your life blood to every area of your body to nourish, balance and heal you physically. The heart coupled with your breath can bring a sense of relaxation to the body as you slow your heart rate and create a pause in your busy mind with each conscious breath you take. When you are consciously aware of your breath, you are actually feeling the human energy system shifting in your body, and you are controlling it.

With the next breath, I want you to begin to activate some thoughts and feelings about your life. Begin to think of the things that you appreciate and are grateful for. You can take your time and don't make it difficult. You may love the morning sunrise or evening sunset, a person, a pet, eating ice cream or watching your favourite movie. As you activate these thoughts of appreciation and gratitude, take note of how your physical body is responding. Do you feel an opening in your heart, a tingling or expansion of the energy around you? Do you feel an emotion that is delicious and you want more of? Just notice.

Breathe, take note and remember how you feel when you breathe into your heart, opening yourself up to feelings of gratitude for your life. This is important. That feeling is real and authentic. The feeling is your "essential self" when you are connected to the good things in your life. I want to emphasize the importance of connecting with whatever you are feeling. Feelings are real, whereas a thought is just energy moving through your "mind." How the thought makes you feel is the message, and if you are paying attention (self-awareness), you can control how you want to feel versus getting lost in the thought of what is making you feel that way. If it doesn't feel good, then it is time for you to take a breath and shift into an energy that feels better, gentler and easier for you.

Feelings are real, whereas a thought is just energy moving through your "mind." How the thought makes you feel is the message, and if you are paying attention (self-awareness), you can control how you want to feel.

Personally, I do this breathing exercise daily. The number of times depends on the number of situations in which I need to shift my energy from something that has me feeling not that great to something that feels better. Remember, I said this book is for anyone who wants to learn how to move from a difficult situation to a less difficult one. Well, this is the gift of your breath as it connects you to your heart. This is self-awareness.

The breath is the gateway to consciousness and brings a person into the present moment. The breath creates the pause between thoughts where all the magic lies. To get connected with yourself, not your ego, you have to stop the mind chatter in your head. In his book *The Untethered Soul*, Michael Singer calls this mind chatter the roommate in your head. I call your awareness of the "roommate in your head" your conscious "self" or the "observer" of your thoughts.

The mental chatter is part of our subconscious mind's ability to pull out data and information from past experiences without us paying attention. As the subconscious processes millions of bits of data, our mind cycles in a frenzy to try to bring order to the chaos going on in our heads. The only tool we have to stop this is our conscious awareness that our minds have run amok, and it is time to "take a breath." This breath pauses the voice or ego mind so that you can observe the thoughts and decide what needs to be done to handle the current situation without interference or distraction from past subconscious programs. Your breath connects you to the quiet stillness of your heart when you activate the connection with thoughts that are calm, ordered and focused on what you want to experience versus habits or patterns developed from the past.

Let me use the example of my client Jane who wanted to improve her relationship with her husband. Every day for weeks my client focused her thoughts on all the things that she appreciated and felt grateful for about her husband. Every time her mind would take her into the past and have her reliving an angry moment or a memory that triggered a difficult feeling, she would take a breath and pause her busy mind to stop the frenzied "roommate" (Singer, 2007) in her head who was trying to get her to revert to the old habit of being critical and angry.

Jane was giving her "self" time to pause and become self-aware. By regulating her breath, she was able to create a sense of calmness and clarity so that she could watch the thoughts cycle through her mind. She would breathe into her heart until her thoughts of appreciation and gratitude would shift her energy, getting her out of her head and into her heart where her true "self" was present. Jane discovered that her response to her husband then became more appropriate and not burdened by past behaviours that were no longer relevant.

The result of becoming self-aware allowed Jane to be much more patient and compassionate towards her husband and his mood as she listened and acknowledged his situation. She realized that what he felt was personal to him, and she didn't have to take it personally. She learned that whatever he projected or blamed on her was not about her. It actually was his pain showing up, and if she could just hold the space without judgment, his energy would move through her without it shifting her out of her energy. Jane learned that when her energy began to drop, she would have to set a boundary with her husband and explain to him that she would not continue a conversation if he wasn't treating her with respect and kindness, and she would do the same for him. She made her intention clear to her husband that she wanted to improve their relationship by honouring each other's differences and finding common ground to work out any of the issues that would come between them.

Over time, Jane also shared that her husband began to shift his behaviour and do the same for her. Remember the Law of the Circle. The energy you put out will come back to you. In this example, the experience of shifting energy was real and set the stage for my client to use this technique in other areas of her life.

When you focus on what you want to experience versus what you don't want, you are giving your "self "the opportunity to live your best life by creating the energetic field around you and for it to be attracted back to you.

When you focus on what you want to experience versus what you don't want, you are giving your "self "the opportunity to live your best life by creating the energetic field around you and for it to be attracted back to you. Hence, knowing "self "is key. The acorn only thought it was an acorn until its shell cracked open. Once the seed of its potential met all the conditions required to become its true nature, then and only then did it grow into a mighty oak. Knowing yourself suggests that you need to let go of your protective "shell" and become open and vulnerable in order to awaken to the untapped potential within. Connecting with your "self" by activating your "heart energy" through the use of your breath is a key to unlocking this potential.

If I asked you right now what you wanted in all areas of your life in order to live your best life, how would you answer? Think about this. Maybe even take a moment to write down whatever pops into your mind. If you find yourself in a state of knowing you want things to change but you don't know how to do it, then the next few pages of this book may be helpful.

One of the exercises that helped me get in touch with my "self" at a deeper level than the persona I presented to the world was an exercise offered in Stephen Covey's books, *The Seven Habits of Highly Effective People* and *First Things First*. For me, the exercise was truly transformational, and I highly recommend you get these books and do the exercise, as described briefly below.

The exercise asks the reader to imagine themself at their own funeral. You are sitting at the back of church, and all of your loved ones are present. The pastor invites family and friends to step up and share what they loved most about "you."

The next step in the exercise is for "you" to identify at least eight meaningful relationships in your life that covered all areas of influence. These would include parents, siblings, friends, teachers, bosses, colleagues, community connections, spiritual or religious people, among others. Once selected, you write down their name and relationship to you and then write down what you would want them to say about you in the event of your passing.

When I did this exercise, I was at a "First Things First" seminar offered by my employer as part of my human resource training. I had read several of Stephen Covey's business books and felt they were amazing as they translated into your personal life as well.

The seminar was well attended with over 100 participants. We sat at tables of five people, all looking towards the front of the room. When we started the exercise, you could hear chatter and voices as people exchanged words. However, as we got into the exercise, the room started to quiet. Everyone was focused on writing and you could almost hear a pin drop. Then slowly you could hear a sniffle and a cough, and

I for one was reaching in my bag for a tissue. I was so moved by what I was writing. I had listed people like my mother, father, spouse, child, sibling, teacher, co-worker, boss, pastor and best friend.

The type of things I wanted them to say about me was to indicate that I was a good person and that they were proud to have known me. I was in tears. Words I wanted to hear were proud, honoured, loved, appreciated, valued, honest, trustworthy, kind, loving, dedicated, hard-working, integrity, compassionate, caring, to name a few.

The tears came when I realized with each word I wrote down was a responsibility to claim ownership of that quality. When everyone finished the work, there was a short break and we all quietly sat and reflected on what we had written.

The next part of the exercise became a question. Are you the person that possesses the qualities that you want to be remembered by? We were all asked to sit and contemplate this question and go through each quality listed and say "yes I am," or "I could be better" or "no I am not." Once this was completed, we were asked to come up with a personal mission, vision and value statement about who we most wanted to be.

Self-awareness is about having a compass or an internal GPS system that will always take you home.

As the seminar leaders explained to us, my vision statement was meant to guide me daily on being the person or my essential self in all of my interactions and responsibilities. The statement that I wrote down on that day over 25 years ago is my North Star or "internal guidance system." Like the North Star that guides you directionally to your destination, this vision statement reminds me when I am not being true to my "self" and to reset the compass and get back on course. Self-awareness is about having a compass or an internal GPS system that will always take you home.

Knowing your "self" means you need to have a vision for what you want to be. For me, being kind, caring, loving, compassionate, funny, honest and trustworthy, and having integrity all became a daily practice in my life.

All of these traits have to be True North. There is only one True North, so either you are the trait or quality or you are not. For example, either you can be kind or you are not, there is no in-between. It is like Gandhi's quote: "Be that which you want to experience in the world." If you want to be treated with kindness, then you must be kind. This is the laws of energy working perfecting. What you radiate you magnetize. As I said earlier, there is no in-between. This information and knowledge relate back to what you learned about intention and the Law of the Circle.

If your intention is to be a certain quality, then you must embody that quality and become it before it will be reflected back to you in relationships. For example, in my healing practice, many of my clients struggled with the idea of being loved. Learning that you have to be "love" to attract love became knowledge that transformed lives. The desire to seek love outside yourself meant that if you didn't love yourself first, it would be unlikely that you would attract it into your life.

If you are seeking love outside yourself and you do not love yourself, the ability to attract that love is diminished.

The above exercise will assist anyone to connect with the energy of the heart and discover the parts of them that may have gone missing while unconsciously living a life too busy to focus on "self." The importance of awakening the love in you is the next essential condition that will guide you to live your best life by rediscovering your "self" through love.

SELF-LOVE

Having a conversation about "self-love" is an important step towards living your best life. Remember when I said "begin with the end in mind"? Self-love is an important beginning to take on your journey to living your best life. If you don't love you, based on the laws of energy, how would it be possible for someone else to love you back? Think about this. If you are seeking love outside yourself and you do not love yourself, the ability to attract that love is diminished.

Take a breath. This part of the book is central to the message I want to convey to you, the reader. Let's do the exercise again where we breathe into the heart and activate thoughts of appreciation and gratitude. Do this right now as you are reading. I want you to get out of your busy monkey mind while you breathe. Drop into the energy of your heart. Calm, relax and open to what it feels like to be in your heart energy. If you practise this technique over time, you will find that simply setting the intention to go into your heart is enough to get you there with just one breath. Practise as often as you can to move out of the "crazy" in your head and into the expansive love in your heart.

If you are with me now, then I will continue to focus on the importance of knowing your "self" and loving yourself. This is huge. What if I told you right here, right now that your true nature is LOVE? How does that make you feel? Do you believe it? Let's investigate this more deeply.

Take a moment right now and think of a newborn baby. Most people would agree that the perfection and beauty of this new life is beyond words for most, especially the family who receives this new life into their world. Most babies were conceived in love, received in love and surrounded in love from the moment they appeared. The true nature of that child is love, just like you were when you were born.

The question that may come to mind is this: if that is true, then why do so many of us feel unlovable or unloved? An answer that I have discovered in my own research is that we separated from this state of being or knowing as part of the process of growing up. I only have to watch my young grandchildren to see the perfection and joy that they are as they learn and discover the world around them. A child at play is creative and joyful. They express themselves without limitation or fear. As they begin to grow, you can notice them taking on the nuances of the family as their facial expressions mimic and make you laugh. A child picks up their cues from their surroundings. Eventually the beliefs of their environment begin to shape the child's world, and the connection to their true essence begins to diminish as they too learn to toe the line and follow the rules of the collective.

The greatest gift we can give ourselves right now is to try to remember what it felt like to be in the midst of our child-like wonder and the perfection we possessed when we took our first breath. For anyone who is a grandparent, you will get this point. Grandchildren come at a time in our life when most of us are getting ready to step off the wheel of "crazy" as it relates to career, raising family and financial burdens. When you hold your grandchild, the burden of responsibility is no longer yours. Your responsibility is only to love them and let their parents deal with the rest of the issues in raising these amazing humans. This is perfect.

The release from responsibility frees a grandparent to be fully present and at play with these amazing beings of pure love and potential. As you watch them at play, you can reflect and connect with their process of discovery and fun. This can lead to moments that open your heart and reconnect you to the part of you that you may have left behind in the busyness of life and the need to fill the roles you felt were expected of you. My grandchildren reminded me of my true nature and gave me the gift of being able to turn back time and let go of all the stuff of life that had me stuck, stalled and ill at ease with the life I had created.

Not all of you have reached your golden years or grandparenthood to experience this shift. But you can know yourself and know that your true nature is love. The power to shift your current situation into a different energy and perspective gives you the freedom to be your "self." All the restrictions and fear you placed on yourself to be something that you "thought" was expected of you is no longer necessary or required. You can be vulnerable and happy in your life by simply loving the person that you are right now, in this very moment. You don't have to be a child or a grandparent, you just have to be you and love that you just the way "you" are.

Take a breath. Take in this information and ask yourself, "Are you willing to embody the idea of loving yourself in order to live your best life?" Think about this. Can you honestly say that you love yourself? If you can and your heart is full and open and life is good, then you are right where you need to be. This is your authenticity showing up and revealing the beauty of yourself and your spirit as you live life fully. However, if you are struggling with looking at yourself in the mirror and loving what is being reflected back at you, you still have some work to do.

Unfortunately, many of my clients often began this work believing they loved themselves only to discover that it was a mask of wishful thinking. The truth was the person they treated the harshest in their life was themself. The emotional traumas you have had throughout your life leave imprints on your energy body and will often short circuit your ability to connect with your essential self. Your being is buried under the heaviness of life happening around you.

This leads to you creating a protective mask to hide your shortcomings and perceived flaws in order to survive and thrive in the world that you are a part of. In the end, you lose touch with the loving energy of your heart, where the true blueprint of your natural talents, gifts and genius are stored. This is where they will wait for "you" until "you" are re-awakened by some event or "take a breath" moment that pushes you to question what you thought you knew about yourself and the world. My intention is to share this knowledge with you now so that you do not have to go through a catastrophic event, dark night of the soul, illness or injury to get your attention.

Learning to love "you" with all the flaws and perceived imperfections that you think you have is not an easy task.

Now is the time for your curiosity to be ignited so that you can reconnect to your purpose and passions. This is when you start to pay attention to the stirring in your heart as you finally awaken to the truth and power of loving your "self." My hope is that the contents of this book might be a catalyst for you to reconnect to the parts of you that you may have forgotten. Learning to love "you" with all the flaws and perceived imperfections that you think you have is not an easy task. However, it is worth the effort and the daily practice of looking in the mirror and telling your reflection that you love what you see no matter what.

Most of us separate from the truth that love is the answer and find other strategies to move forward in our life. So many of us disconnect from our heart energy and live completely in our heads. Although there are moments and memories of wonderful experiences, many of those are forgotten as we try to navigate through the day-to-day busyness of trying to survive and thrive in a world that can be overwhelming.

I read in David Hawkins book *Power versus Force* that if we were to break down the percentage of our consciousness into the areas of our life that we focus our attention and intention on, it would break down as follows: 10 per cent of our consciousness is focused on the good things in our life (positivity); 60 per cent is on the things that aren't working in our life (negativity); and the remaining 30 per cent is the numbness of being stuck in our life.

When I first read these statistics, I was shocked. However, after thinking about them, I realized they were true. Start a conversation with someone and often the first thing they will mention is how lousy the weather is or how lousy their life seems to be. It is the rare person you meet who is a beam of sunshine and wants to talk about the great things going on in their life and the world. It is almost like there is a contest to see who has the worst life and experiences to share.

The first step in believing in yourself and loving yourself is to accept yourself just the way you are and work daily at the qualities that you want to be.

After I read those statistics, I set a goal and intention for myself moving forward. I was going to work on the 30 per cent of untapped potential and the 60 per cent of negativity to move those numbers towards improving the parts of my life that I was grateful for and appreciated. I was on the path to consciousness through the process of learning to love my "self" and live my best life.

Now I want you to go back and think about that vision, mission and values statement that can be your guidance system to become your true or essential self. If you want happy in the world and in your life, you have to be happy. If you want success in your life, you have to believe you are successful, no matter the outcome of whatever you do. The principle is to believe that whatever you need or want in your life, you already possess it. You have it within you to activate. The first step in believing in yourself and loving yourself is to accept yourself just the way you are and work daily at the qualities that you want to be.

Remember the saying "fake it until you become it." Begin this process by activating the wants in your life so that you can deactivate the do not wants in your life. If you act the way you want to experience the world, the universe will notice and begin to move energy in your direction to support that want. The laws of energy are scientific to the letter so whatever you radiate you will magnetize. When you radiate "self" love, you will magnetize "more love" back to you. This is a scientific law of energy, whether you believe it or not. It is truth.

The great mystery of the universe is simply these laws. The "universe" gives you exactly what you ask for, whether it is conscious or unconscious. Therefore, clearing out the old beliefs and programs is the easiest way to do this. Focusing and paying attention to the things you love about yourself and your life will shift the energy to support what you want versus what you don't want.

> ***The "universe" gives you exactly what you ask for, whether it is conscious or unconscious.***

There is no need for self-improvement or modification of the current you; there is simply a requirement for you to change your mind about your true nature. If you can accept that you are love and all that you think, say, do, feel and believe come from a place of love, then your life with take on a whole new light and direction.

When you are stuck in old programs and beliefs, you are like a hamster on a hamster wheel running like crazy and getting nowhere. When your mind and heart are disconnected, the energy of love can't reach your mind to calm the feeling of overwhelm that takes over your life. You will keep repeating the same habits and patterns that keep you stuck, much like the hamster on its wheel.

Take a breath now. When you breathe, you stop the hamster wheel, you slow the energy, you calm the heart rate, and you can begin to clear your mind and allow the energy of your heart to guide your thoughts. Pause and allow. When you can see what you are thinking as the observer of your thoughts rather than being lost in thought, you can shift the feeling of overwhelm into something different. Shifting from a difficult situation to a less difficult one is simply the process of dropping into your heart energy and giving yourself permission to appreciate and to be grateful for what is working in your life. What is working in your life is what you want more of, so your attention and intention focused on this energy will create new opportunities to open up.

To love yourself is to put yourself first. If you are out of alignment with you, how can you possibly align with anything else in your life in a meaningful way? Think about this.

Most people are familiar with the pre-flight safety demonstration on an airplane. However, if you are not, let me explain it in an attempt to clarify the meaning of self-love. Stewards on an airplane give safety instructions that you should follow in case of an emergency. You are to put your oxygen mask on first to ensure your safety so that you are able to help others who may need your help. This is especially true if you are travelling with young children or the elderly, who may need assistance. If you don't put your mask on before you assist them, you could pass out before you have time to help them. This concept is hugely important to grasp.

To love yourself is to put yourself first.

This safety tip can be an analogy for our energy: you cannot give out energetically that which you do not have. Conversely, the way the laws of energy work is you cannot receive energy that you do not already possess. Using love as a frequency of energy, if you don't love yourself (oxygen mask), how can you give love to another (oxygen)? Conversely, if someone is sending love to you (oxygen), if you do not possess it (oxygen mask), how can you receive it? It basically means that you are running on empty most of the time if you don't take care of yourself first.

SELF-CARE

The discussion about self-care follows self-love, as I wanted to be able to show that both go hand-in-hand. Self-love is digging deep and uncovering all of the qualities of your being that make you want to get up in the morning and live your best life. Self-care is ensuring that your energy "love tank" is always full.

In my practice, most of my clients came to me tapped out, worn out, beaten down and stuck in a situation or experience that they could not find their way out of. The clients wondered if the work that I do as an energy practitioner could help them to uncover whatever was contributing or causing them to be in the physical, mental, emotional or spiritual pain that they were in. Some clients came with physical pain, while others would be stuck in relationship drama, financial concerns or other assorted issues.

I always answered by saying that whatever work we did together would rely on their willingness to look at some of their subconscious beliefs and emotional traumas from their past that might be contributing to the "issues in their tissues." Please note that my philosophy in working with anyone depended on their "will" and commitment to do the work required and necessary to shift the energy that was preventing them from living their best life.

> ***Self-care is ensuring that your energy "love tank" is always full.***

The self-care portion was a difficult concept to understand for many. My female clients in particular were taught and raised in environments where their responsibility was to take care of others, so putting themselves first was not an option. The feminine energy that has been passed down generationally has left an imprint in the energy field of most women that has emphasized the importance of being selfless versus selfish.

This pattern played out in my own life, and as I began working with other women, I discovered that it was an inherent belief carried in many feminine energy fields. History had taught many females that being selfish would get them punished or shamed. Parents would often reinforce this belief and outcome as well. I am sure some of you must remember as a child being chastised or punished for not sharing your toys with a sibling or other child and conversely praised and rewarded when you did. The messaging was clear for a child: mommy and daddy love me when I share, and they get mad at me when I don't so that must mean they do not love me when they get mad.

As I have explained before, the subconscious programs built around a child's experience will develop belief systems that will support behaviours that are deemed good and bad simply based on how their parents reinforce or praise them. You can imagine how this type of reinforcement would create a belief over time. That is, being selfless was good and therefore you would be loved, and conversely to be selfish was bad and you would lose love.

Many women shared with me how, as children, they played the role of the good girl and people pleaser to receive love and affection from others. They also shared how judgmental they were of women who appeared to be selfish because they had more freedom to do "selfish" things, like taking care of themselves through attention to things they loved in their life. It seemed like they were caught in a values conflict. To be caring and supportive of others meant that they could not be caring and supportive of themselves. The voice in their head said, "If I am caring and supportive of others, I am judged to be good, and if I take care of myself, I am judged to be bad. Therefore, I must be good to be loved."

The feminine energy that has been passed down generationally has left an imprint in the energy field of most women that has emphasized the importance of being selfless versus selfish.

This belief and value statement repeated itself throughout much of my client base. It was too much of a repeat pattern to be ignored. As I focused on what factors contributed to the development of this behavioural pattern, I discovered that each client had specific "emotional" traumas or memories of the past that was the catalyst for the good girl to manifest in their persona. Being able to uncover the memories of the emotional traumas allowed my clients to see how as a child they had formulated the habit and over time it became an automatic response to care for others to receive the love that they needed.

Many of these women felt that they had lost touch with "who" they were and what they were meant to do in their life. One client shared her despair. I will call this client Susan to protect her identity. Her story started with how powerless she felt in her relationship and that she had no boundaries of her own and was constantly making herself small so everyone else could be big. Much of her story reflected how she had been the good girl: people pleasing, a selfless and kind person, and everyone else took advantage of her goodness. She felt like she had dug a hole and couldn't find her way out.

After many sessions and emotional releases, using the Emotion and Body Code method along with Psych-K protocols, we were able to uncover her patterns and beliefs. (Please note: I discuss these healing modalities in Chapter 4, under Foundational Requirement for Health). As Susan's self-awareness or conscious mind became aware of these patterns, she began to take responsibility for the role she played in becoming the "mask" or ego persona of the good girl and in her words "a door mat." Her acceptance that the source of her power depended on her focusing on what she needed and wanted in her life was a huge shift for Susan and began to transform her experience. These are my notes following the session in which Susan had turned a corner in her healing process:

> *"Susan was a different person this week. She opened up the session by stating, 'I am focusing on me, now.' She shared a few stories of how she handled a few situations this week that were completely different from how she would have behaved from the past. She looked and sounded happy and very much in the flow of her personal power. She talked about wanting to take some courses to better understand the use of her digital camera. She talked about some great ideas on how to use this talent and ended with 'my heart's desire is to be independent. I have always been attached to others and never felt safe with my own abilities and this is about to change.'"*

The shift Susan experienced in this example had followed many weeks of learning to connect with her heart through her breath, staying present and allowing herself to feel the part of her that had chosen to give her power away to others. She was able to let the memories and the beliefs behind those memories release from her energy field, and she replaced them with new beliefs and ideas about herself. She stopped blaming others for her situation and took on the huge task of pulling back her power through the daily practice of noticing when she would be triggered into her old habits.

When Susan decided to become more selfish, she discovered herself again. She connected with her heart and was able to expand her "heart's desire" into actionable intentions that she could take responsibility for. Her self-awareness and self-love had grown, and she knew that being selfish was the self-care key that was required to open the door to the next best part of her life.

The most important message in connecting to self through awareness, love and care is to understand the mechanism that separated us from the ability to do this in the first place. We lost the connection to the energy of our heart, and our subconscious mind became the driving force that began to create our perception of life and how we chose to experience that life. It is only through reconnecting with our hearts that we will be able to find our "essential self."

Heart connection is the pathway to knowing yourself and healing your life. When you separate from the heart you cannot "see," "feel" and "believe" in the person who is being reflected back to you in the mirror. This is when you will lose yourself and the power to be in charge of your life and the experiences that will keep you in the flow of your dreams and passions.

Heart connection is the pathway to knowing yourself and healing your life.

It is simply reconnecting to the heart and using your conscious mind to guide your decision-making each and every day that will bring you back to your authenticity and true nature, which is love. The subconscious mind will naturally provide input. Some of it will be awesome and needed; however, most of it is not required. Life is about living each moment to the fullest and then moving on to the next moment without cluttering your energy with mind chatter, judgments, past experiences and emotions that are not serving you.

It is much like being a passenger in a car. If you are staring out the window at the scenery going by and you notice its beauty, it leaves an impression and you move on to the next impression. However, if you see something and it grabs your attention and you get lost in thought over what you witness, you will miss what is ahead of you on the road. Life is like that. If we can be present in the moment we are experiencing, we can move through whatever is happening—good, bad or indifferent—allowing it to be what it is and not letting it slow down, block or stall our ability to continue with the flow of life.

Self-awareness, care and love are about you focusing on what is necessary and important in the present and allowing all the other stuff to move through you to create balance and harmony with whatever shows up in your life. Much like the scenery passing you by on the road, take it in and then move on to the next part of the road. If you need to stop and take a longer look, that is okay, but eventually you will have to get back in the vehicle and continue your journey.

The challenges, the ups and the downs are all part of the journey, and as a passenger, you can notice and allow all of life to show up and then let it flow without it disrupting or interrupting your ability to live your best life. Knowing your "self" makes you responsible for your "energy" so that you can focus on the good things in your life with the added benefit of being a positive influence on the people around you.

Understanding the energy connection to the physical body is information I hope will motivate you to do your healing work through the processes outlined in this book. Please know I do not have medical training. I have knowledge and experience of how energy is activated in the physical body and how the movement of that energy impacts our health and wellness.

Let me share a personal story of healing to highlight why this information became important to me. In 2002, two years after my husband's near-fatal illness, our family went on a vacation to relax and reward ourselves for surviving and thriving through a very difficult two years of healing for my husband and my family as a whole. It was a wonderful trip, and we all enjoyed the sun, fun and playtime. My husband in particular felt rejuvenated, and he shared with me that he was finally at a place where he felt he got his life back.

My relief and joy were beyond words. However, what surprised me was how my physical body responded to his news. As he sat across from me and said, "I feel like myself again—I'm back!" my body let down. I felt my energy plummet, and a fatigue and ache started to spread through my body. By the time I got home at the end of the week, I had developed a respiratory infection and I was headed to the doctors. For the next several months, I was on three or more rounds of antibiotics, none of which seemed to get to the root cause of my issues.

It felt like all my body systems were shutting down. Not only did I have respiratory issues, my digestive system started to fail me. My immune system was so compromised that I ended up with strep throat and bronchitis. Finally, my family doctor (God bless him) sat me down and laid things out for me. He said that I had completely exhausted my body over the two-year period I cared for my husband and family. He explained to me how the stress of the ordeal had tapped me out and compromised my immune system and that by not taking care of myself I had compromised my own health. He was so wise. He ended up talking to my family, and each one of them was given instructions on how to support me to get me back onto my feet.

We have already covered the importance of self-care so it does not need to be repeated here. Unless you recognize and experience a health crisis that highlights the importance of self-care, you may never get the message to put yourself first (oxygen mask on). This was a huge lesson for me.

It was through my recovery process that I spent time reflecting on my health situation and asked the deep question, "What could I have done differently?" At the time of my illness, I was training in reflexology and working with a spiritual/life coach. Both of these teachers/mentors helped me to focus on my self-care. My family also stepped up to support me, and within a year I was back on my feet. I was much wiser and had learned a valuable lesson about the human energy system and the healing process. It was an inside-out job and I had firsthand knowledge and experience of what that involved. This is when I began to focus my attention and intention to learn as much as I could to heal myself and through the process assist others who may be going through what I had.

Another important event in my life that deserves to be shared is a story of another health crisis I had when I was 20. At that time, I did not understand nor did I connect with putting myself first. The story begins with my then family doctor guiding me through a diagnostic process to try to uncover the issues I was having, and in the end there was nothing medically wrong with me in terms of illness or disease. However, what he explained to me was that the "stress" of my life was contributing to the debilitating pain I was experiencing in my stomach. He was the first doctor to explain the parasympathetic and sympathetic nervous systems to me.

If you are not familiar with these terms, I will explain them briefly as they are both essential in maintaining balance and harmony in our physical body to sustain our health and wellness. This knowledge will assist you in understanding the importance of your self-awareness in being able to move from one state of being to another by understanding these two nervous systems.

The sympathetic nervous system is our "fight or flight" response to life situations. Our brain has a communication network that signals the rest of the body when we need to react to the stressors of life. The sympathetic nervous system basically prepares us to manage the "stress" by shutting down all of our body systems so that the "energy" in our bodies will go to our extremities so we can "run" like heck away from "predators" who will surely cause our demise. This is part of what is referred to as the "reptilian brain," which unfortunately has not evolved to the time frame we now live in. The brain does not realize that most of the current stress of our lives does not require us to "fight or flight." Instead, our stress comes from trying to survive in a world that has placed so many demands on us to meet the requirements of our day-to-day living.

My doctor from many years ago explained that the pain in my stomach was my sympathetic nervous system taking control of my life due to the many demands I was trying to juggle at the time. I was in university, had a part-time job, had just gotten engaged and didn't have any idea how to juggle it all. The stress and pressures in my life were wreaking havoc with my digestive system as it had been shut down to deal with my "fight and flight" signal from the brain.

The parasympathetic nervous system receives communication from the brain that all is well in our life. It allows all body systems to function normally in balance and harmony with the requirements necessary to stay healthy. Of course, the parasympathetic system will only run smoothly when "issues in our tissues" that disturb this delicate balance are not obstructing it.

My doctor explained that in order for my stomach issues to be brought under control, I needed to focus my attention on what was necessary and important and not let the feeling of overwhelm take over. He explained that the "feeling" of overwhelm created the stress, and the stress caused my sympathetic nervous system to be triggered into "fight or flight" and then the pain would follow. When I remember this talk now, 40 years later, he was the one that started me to think more deeply about how much I could actually control in my life. Unfortunately, it took me many more years to connect the dots and actually take control of my life and experiences. However, the strategies he taught me back then are a mirror to what I am sharing in the pages of this book.

His advice at the time was to try to avoid the "trigger" response by using techniques to stay in my parasympathetic nervous system. He suggested breathing techniques and staying present. I will admit that this helped me a great deal. First, I knew there was nothing medically wrong with me, and second, he gave me advice on how I could manage the pain if I paid attention. Little did I know this advice would be part of the fuel that shifted my life goals towards the work I do today.

Now that you are fully focused on your "self," the last condition that is essential for your potential to flourish and grow is to understand "emotional energies" and how they impact our ability to connect with our heart and create our best life. Emotions are feelings. Feelings are real and they need our undivided attention when they are triggered.

Emotions are feelings. Feelings are real and they need our undivided attention when they are triggered.

Condition 6. EMOTIONS: a strong feeling deriving from one's circumstances, mood, or relationship with others (*Oxford Dictionary*)

The important message in understanding our EMOTIONS as a condition to live our best life is accepting that emotional energies exist in our human energy fields as a scale of frequencies or feelings, similar to the notes on a musical scale or the colours on a colour wheel. All of our emotions/feelings exist within the human energy field to be used to create our life experience. This is similar to a musician using the notes on a musical scale to write a song or a painter to use the colour wheel to produce their art through selection and mixing of the colours. Not every piece of music uses the notes the same way or even uses all of them at the same time. A painter also can use a variety of colours to represent the grass or a tree, and each painter is unique in their expression. Understanding this concept frees you to see that emotions/feelings, like sounds and colours, can be chosen to create an experience.

The energy/frequency of an emotion is a FEELING. This is important to understand. Emotion is a feeling that we get in response to whatever is happening in our life. Somewhere along the line, we have decided that some emotions are good and some are bad.

In the discussion about self-care, the emotions of self-less versus selfish have been used as an example of how "being" and "expressing" both of these emotions is important in our life. To take care of yourself, a.k.a. selfish, means on the level of energy that you are filling your tank with whatever it is that you need so that when you go out into the world, you have a full tank of energy. If you are self-less without being selfish first, then you run the risk of running on empty with the danger of becoming tapped out and worn out and in some cases become physically ill as your body systems have been depleted of the life force energy they need to survive and thrive.

Understand, know and believe that emotions are NOT good or bad; they are simply feelings in our human energy system/life force energy. It is through conscious/subconscious mind that these emotions are activated and used to create experiences for us. This is where your self-care is critically important. If your emotions have dulled your ability to connect with your heart and feel the joy in your life, it means on some level you have made a decision to

> ***Emotions are NOT good or bad; they are simply feelings in our human energy system/ life force energy.***

disconnect from the fullness of your life by giving your energy away with no back-up plan.

Let me give you a personal example of how this played out in my life. I had been working with Kristina Jansz, a life coach/spiritual teacher, who said to me in one of my sessions, "Sharon, you do know that it is okay to feel emotions?" It struck me as such an odd thing to say. I quickly responded that of course I allowed myself to feel things, and she simply replied, "Are you sure of that?" She asked me to spend time thinking about how I handled my emotions in my day-to-day life.

That afternoon, I was preparing dinner and my middle daughter, who was about 15 at time, was sitting at the dinner table doing her homework. I was thinking about emotions and what my coach had said. I nonchalantly asked my daughter if she thought I expressed my feelings or emotions well. Without even blinking an eye or even looking at me, she just laughed and said, "Mom, no one ever knows what you are feeling. You always have a smile on your face and you try to make others feel good so I wouldn't have a clue what you really feel."

I was stunned. I thought I was this person who was in touch with her feelings, and out of the mouth of one of my most trusted and loved relationships was a truth I was not prepared for. She was right. I absolutely would never let anyone see my vulnerability or the pain I felt emotionally. I would stuff down and block the flow of my feelings so that I never made anyone else feel uncomfortable. In doing so, I was going through the motions of living and not truly in touch with myself and what was important to me.

If we do not connect with the authenticity of what we feel and allow it to move through us, it will get "stuck" in us.

It was shortly after this exchange that I really began to do the work to reconnect with my dreams and the vision I had for my life. Somewhere along the line, I unconsciously chose to believe that I didn't matter. I had to learn to love myself and put myself first. By doing this, I was more authentic and real not only to myself but to my family and those in my field of influence. With three young daughters, I knew that playing the role of a victim and martyr was not something they needed to learn or witness. By loving myself and focusing on what I wanted in my life, I shifted my energy into a new frequency. I was teaching my children to focus on what they wanted and to know that they were worth it.

The way the laws of energy work in simple terms is that "you can't give (energetically) what you don't have, and you can't have (energetically) what you don't give. Remember the oxygen mask analogy? This is the scientific law of "cause and affect" in action. The reason I bring this up again is that emotions are feelings, and feelings are real. If we do not connect with the authenticity of what we feel and allow it to move through us, it will get "stuck" in us.

Take a breath. This is huge. The power of who you are and what you experience is based on how you connect with the emotional energies you have available to you.

On a scale of emotions, each emotion has an energy frequency/feeling that will take you from the lowest vibrating to the highest vibrating energy within the energy fields of our body. The lowest frequency emotion would be "fear." Within the frequency of fear, emotions create feelings like resentment, jealousy, hopelessness, yearning, longing, helplessness, shame, bitterness, anger, frustration, self-abuse, shock, unworthy, worthless, guilt, confusion, discouragement, despair, betrayal, anxiety, depression, abandonment, conflict and many more.

The highest vibrating emotion within our energy field is love. Within the frequency of love, emotions create feelings like joy, bliss, happiness, peace, calm, balance, beauty, laughter, worth, value, honour, trust, integrity, kindness, compassion, empathy, excitement, humour, awe, wonder, generosity, gratitude, appreciation and many more. Looking at the scale of emotions and understanding that labelling them as good or bad is a "personal" judgment and an oversimplified way to "file" the emotions away, especially if our subconscious mind gets hold of the belief behind the emotion. The example I shared with you above had me stuck in the "fear-based" emotions of a victim and martyr. Being stuck in these beliefs had me spinning my wheels and feeling disconnected from the joy I should have been feeling in my life with all the blessings that I had been given.

Remember the difference between selfless and selfish. Selfless was deemed good, but it separated the self from caring and nurturing itself, creating a disconnection to the heart, so the self was no longer in touch with its purpose and passion in life. That is exactly what I was feeling when my daughter challenged me with her perspective of my behaviour.

Selfish was labelled bad. I have since discovered that when I become selfish for all the right reasons, which is self-care, selfish healed and opened my heart to the greater possibilities and opportunities that existed outside of serving others. I realized that the shift I had to make was in my perception of what each of these emotions represented to me. In my story, I had to learn to say no to other people's yeses and to say yes to my own. That was the beginning of my personal transformation and healing journey.

The discussion that focused on self-care was to emphasize the importance of knowing that what we focus our attention on will become our experience or reality. The experience, as you can see, is a choice. Do you choose the low-frequency emotions or the higher frequency emotions to move towards what you want to experience?

Again, in the story I shared with you, when I said I changed frequencies through self-care and love, I meant that I shifted into what I wanted to feel versus what I did not want to be feeling. I connected with my "breath," dropped into my heart and began to feel joy and love moving through me again. This did not happen overnight. It took time, patience and commitment on my part to be more conscious of what I was feeling so I could decide to shift into a better feeling. Remember, the goal of this information and process is to teach you how to shift from a difficult situation to a less difficult one.

Referring back to the discussion on conscious and subconscious mind, it is important to understand that the conscious mind brings you into self-awareness, whereas the subconscious mind will take you into past experiences to repeat them in the present.

Now that you understand that your emotions create feelings as energy, your conscious mind can pick up the frequency and decide which feeling you would prefer to another. The ability to choose the feeling is where your power comes from. By simply taking a deep breath to pause and then separate from the subconscious mind's function of replaying the reel of past possibilities, you are now in the present and able to see the uncontrolled thoughts that are swirling in your mind.

The self-care component is choosing the emotion/feeling that brings you into the energy of your heart and begins the process of activating a higher vibrating frequency that will calm and relax (parasympathetic nervous system) your energy and make you feel better. The simple act of doing this sets up the process of self-love to step in and take over as you realize that how you feel and experience life is about choosing "you" first before you get lost in the overwhelm that exists outside of you.

To simplify this further, I offer the analogy of light and dark. As you are aware, darkness is simply the absence of light. Watching the sunset in the evening as the day transforms into night is a beautiful illustration of how darkness appears as the moon replaces the sun. If the moon goes behind a cloud, its light is still present, but the darkness of the night intensifies as the light is blocked. It is the same on a rainy or cloudy day. The sunlight is always shining behind the cloud even though we cannot see or feel it.

The goal is to be conscious of the emotions you are feeling so that you can stay on the lighter or neutral side of the scale.

Fear-based emotions would be the shadow-based energies, and love-based emotions would be the light-based energies. Understanding that each emotion has a shadow and light side allows the conscious observer to decide which side of the emotion they want to experience.

I have put together a chart identifying the fear-based/shadow emotions and the love-based/light emotions that are on a scale, much like the emotions of self-ish and self-less. The goal is to be conscious of the emotions you are feeling so that you can stay on the lighter or neutral side of the scale. Refer to the Scale of Emotions below.

Scale of Emotions

Fear-Based Feelings or "Shadow" Emotions	Love-Based Feelings or "Light" Emotions
Fear	trust/faith
inferiority	ability
Pride	humility
inadequate	powerful
Tension	peace
Anxiety	calm
Illness	health
helplessness	empowerment
Lie	truth
poverty	abundance
Greed	generosity
resentment	forgiveness
jealousy	gratitude
criticism	praise
discouragement	encouragement
anger	patience
mean	kind
bully	supportive
trapped	freedom
gossip	helpfulness
weakness	strength
prejudice	oneness
envy	joy
despair	hope
failure	success
bitch	good girl
judgment	discernment

Please note that this chart is only a sample size of the emotions that can create feelings within our human energy systems.

Once you have had a chance to read the list and think about this sampling of emotions, please take a moment to reflect on what it means in the larger context of your understanding of your emotions. Self-awareness is about conscious awareness in the present moment.

Subconscious is also awareness; however, it is automatic without a decision-making process available.

If you are familiar with the yin-yang symbol in Eastern culture, it represents the union of light and dark. The symbol is a circle with one side of the circle light and the other side dark. When each side is in balance, there is harmony. This is a perfect way to represent our emotional energies. If we can experience both emotions in balance, we create a neutrality of feeling. For example, if we activate an emotion of envy, we can sense and feel the shadow, as it is uncomfortable and makes us feel less. On the other hand, the light side of envy is joy, and it feels expansive and wonderful. Once you experience the shadow and light side of emotions, that experience gives you an opportunity through discernment to pick your experience. However, being self-aware and present with how you are feeling is the essential condition.

Using the emotions of envy and joy as an example, let's say you are in a situation in which you hear of your friend's success in landing a new job. You are in the same situation of looking for a new job but have not had any success. You might initially feel envious, as you have been working as hard as your friend with different results. If you notice how envy makes you feel, which is most likely uncomfortable as the nature of your thoughts and physical body respond to the news, then you have a choice to make. Do you want to feel envious or do you want to feel joy for your friend?

Your awareness can shift merely by taking a breath, giving yourself an opportunity to acknowledge the feeling of envy (which, by the way, is natural/normal in this situation; it is not a bad thing—it just is), and then slowly and deliberately breathe until you can shift your breath into your heart to calm your mind and release the emotion. Once you do this, you can shift your thoughts to ones that activate joy for your friend and support you in knowing that what you give in energy to your friend will come back to you through the Law of the Circle. In this example, you used your breath to notice what you were feeling, and then by not judging yourself or your friend as "bad," you let the feeling move through you and be replaced with a kinder and gentler feeling.

This process is very important. If you push the feeling down and do not acknowledge or express it, the feeling will store in your energy field and you will find yourself ruminating about the situation over time. Until you deal with what you are feeling, it will simply stay stuck in your energy systems and prevent your life force energy from flowing freely within your physical body. The feelings that are stored can be come toxic over time, and this is when your health and wellness can become compromised.

The example above demonstrates that when you "feel" (emotion), it is the cue for you to "take a breath" and slow down the subconscious mind's automatic response to whatever is happening. The breath creates the pause so that you can come into the present moment by separating you from your thoughts and allowing you to pay attention to what you are feeling and what your mind is telling you to do about it. The fear-based emotions feel uncomfortable and often will cause your physical body to react.

When you "feel" (emotion), it is the cue for you to "take a breath".

In another example, using the feeling of despair, your body might respond with a feeling like a tightening in your chest, shortness of breath, tears, lethargy or brain fog. Your senses feel dulled and your capacity to move energy is blocked. Subconsciously you might want to curl up in ball and shut yourself off from the rest of the world. However, the conscious mind–when activated through your breath—will allow you to feel the emotion while observing the thoughts attached to it. As you continue the breath work and begin to listen to your internal coach, it will tell you to breathe into your heart and activate a feeling of appreciation and gratitude for anything or everything in your life. This initiates a calmer energy that will clear your mind and open your heart energy. Despair can be released, and you can activate a feeling that is calmer and gentler.

Remember, that in your heart energy you are giving yourself a chance to make a different decision. Hope is always on the other side of despair. The conscious mind will pick up a new feeling tone and begin to sort through solutions to elevate your energy out of despair and into a gentler emotional energy that will feel better.

I had this type of emotional shift several years ago when I volunteered in our community hospice. I provided complementary therapies to the residents to support their comfort in the later part of their end-of-life care. It was a humbling experience and one that taught me so much about service and presence. As part of the ongoing training for staff and volunteers, information workshops were provided to educate us on different conditions we might experience while working with the residents. One particular workshop and presentation had me feeling the depths of "despair" for what was described as a hopeless condition. The disease was ALS, or amyotrophic lateral sclerosis.

When the word hopeless was used, I found myself getting angry. I wanted to shout at the presenters and tell them that without hope how could anyone suffering from this disease find the strength and courage to move forward. As I sat with my thoughts and feelings, I wrote down the word HOPE on my notepad. I stared at the word and read it over and over again. I felt my energy shift out of despair, out of anger, and I began to feel like I was waking up to something bigger. Then I wrote, "Hearts Open Possibilities Enter," that is, H.O.P.E.

The idea that the emotional energy of hope radiates from our heart left me feeling expanded and more connected to the possibility that we are more powerful and capable when we come from love rather than fear. It is heart energy and hope that can move you when you feel beaten down by life. Hope gives you a chance to get yourself back up on your feet so that you can keep going and face life as it meets you each day.

> ***We are more powerful and capable when we come from love rather than fear.***

Do you remember when I said this book is meant for anyone who feels they might be in a difficult situation and they might want to make it less difficult? Well, you have reached the part of the book where this is now possible. You have learned about the breath, conscious/

subconscious mind, intention, energy, self-awareness, self-care, self-love and emotions. When all of these conditions are combined, the opportunity to reflect on how to begin to live your best life from a place of power can be created. When our heart opens and possibility enters (hope), there is nothing that can hold you back.

Chapter Three

NOURISHING THE SEEDS OF YOUR POTENTIAL

Once the seeds of your potential are ready, they must be planted and nurtured in order for them to grow to their full potential. This chapter will outline the process of developing the perfect "soil" for your seeds to grow.

I have mentioned several times that I have worked with clients in a healing practice that focuses on energy and transformation. The catalyst, as mentioned earlier, was the life-changing event of my husband's illness and what I had witnessed in hospital. The pursuit to understand the human energy system/spirit led me on a training mission I would never have dreamt possible unless I was willing to let go of old mindsets that kept me stuck in old thinking.

I was willing to let go of old mindsets that kept me stuck in old thinking.

If you recall, my intention was to figure out what had connected me to that feeling of bliss when I had surrendered in hospital to my husband's condition. The only thing I could relate it to, without sounding crazy, was an unidentified energy that caused the movement of air and the flash of light. My experience of it created a gap in what I thought I knew, and that gap was the opening that led me into the realization that I was not alone. There was definitely something in the "ethers" that surrounded, guided, supported and protected me. Something that felt that amazing wasn't malevolent; it felt loving and inclusive. That feeling led me into the study of spirituality.

The following pages will provide a perspective on spirituality and shifting mindset. The intent of offering this perspective is to illustrate that our health and wellness can be impacted by choosing our experiences through consciousness, care and connection to something greater than ourselves.

SPIRITUALITY AND SHIFTING MINDSET

Religious beliefs and practices around the world have groups of people sharing common connection to a higher power that would offer an explanation for the energy that I felt and saw while in hospital. Common names for this higher power include God, Buddha, Jesus, Allah, Creator, Divine Intelligence, Universal Energy, Source Energy and Jehovah. I have no opinion on how people practise their religion or their belief. I have great respect for those who are passionate and part of a like-minded community to celebrate their belief. However, my belief is based on a personal relationship I have with this "higher power" as it has changed my mind and belief that I am not alone and something greater than myself is guiding me to live my best life.

The common thread that runs through all of us is a "life force energy" that seeks the same thing—the ability to survive and thrive in the world we are born.

This connection to something greater than myself is what I call spirituality, and it has been hugely important in my shift in consciousness. I do not see humanity as separate anymore. I see many of us as different in terms of gender, race, culture, religion or education, but the common thread that runs through all of us is a "life force energy" that seeks the same thing—the ability to survive and thrive in the world we are born.

The study of energy through the various healing modalities I have trained in has taught me that all living organisms are connected at the level of "energy." This connection means that we are one or united at the level of consciousness. Spirituality suggests that this interconnectedness means that our "spirit/life force energy" is connected to the collective energy field of the planet. This understanding is important for each of us so that we can take responsibility for our own energy as we move through our daily life.

The way I understand energy is that everything in the universe is made up of energy, even the space that appears empty between us. The interconnectedness of all things creates a web of communication that allows living organisms to survive and thrive through the use of their senses and the messages received through this web.

If you think of this on a personal level, the energy that moves through you is connected to the energy that surrounds you. The field of energy that surrounds you is part of your personal space. It gives you signals and signs as you move forward in your daily life. The energy you pick up is from all of your senses. What you see, feel, touch, hear, taste and intuit within your field is sending you messages (if you are paying attention) to influence you as you make decisions to support your health, wellness and survival. The energy of the collective, when processed through the heart, represents our connection to something greater than ourselves. The energy of the heart is love, and it is the impulse that first created life on this planet. The ability to tap into this energy gives each one of us mastery over our experience and the power to invoke all that is for our highest and greatest good.

I shared with you the moment of my surrender to the "universe" during my husband's illness. It was not the energy of giving up; it was an energy that I knew was available if I let go of outcome and surrendered in faith and trust to love. Whatever the outcome was to be, I knew that I had done everything possible in my power to support and hold space for my husband. It was now up to whatever the plan was for his life that took over. I knew that whatever happened, I would have the resilience, strength and ability to move through it because I trusted that I was not alone. I was fortunate enough to watch him come back to me, and I know that it is not always the case for everyone who has a loved one challenged with survival. What I learned was that my reaction to the outcome would determine how the rest of my life would unfold. I decided that love and family were my focus and I would stay present and focused on the healing process.

Any practitioner working in the field of energy knows this as a truth. Whenever you are working with a living organism—whether plant, animal or human—you can influence its energy by simply moving into its field or space. The influence a practitioner can exert is through their thoughts, words, actions and belief systems as they work with a client. This work must always be done with permission from the client.

> ***Whenever you are working with a living organism—whether plant, animal or human—you can influence its energy by simply moving into its field or space.***

The interesting thing about energy work is that everyone, not just trained practitioners, has this ability to impact energy fields but they may not be aware of it. The simple truth is that, whether conscious or unconscious, your thoughts, opinions, feelings and beliefs about someone can impact their energy whether it is "intentional" or not. The power of prayer has proven to assist those who are in a healing crisis or loss. The collective energy of many to support, guide and protect those who are in a health crisis or life challenge often has been shown to add strength and courage to those who are challenged. The impact of loving thoughts and prayers can heal.

In Lynn McTaggert's book *The Intention Experiment*, she gives examples of how a scientist performing an experiment can affect the results of that experiment through expectations they may have about the results. This is called the "observer effect," and it is similar to what we call a self-fulfilling prophecy. If you believe it to be true, then it will be. All energy that a human being sends out from their energy field to the collective energy field around them has the ability to impact and alter the energy of another. Remembering that your thoughts are creative is an important awareness to have as you move in the world.

The work of Masaru Emoto, author of *The Hidden Messages in Water* and *The True Power of Water*, also strongly reinforces the idea that human "consciousness" can change the energy field both in and around you. Understanding that the physical body is 70 per cent water is important to know as you read his work and his hypothesis about healing and life balance.

In Mr. Emoto's experiments, he was able to demonstrate that water could understand "words." In one particular experiment, he filled two identical bottles with water. On one bottle he taped the word happiness and the other bottle unhappiness. Both bottles were frozen and then the frozen water was examined under a microscope to see the type of crystal formation that developed. The bottle that had happiness attached to it formed beautiful water crystals, and the other bottle formed broken and unbalanced crystals. It appeared that the water that had unhappy taped to it had tried to create crystals but soon exhausted itself and crashed, happiness never to be achieved.

Emoto did extensive experiments on numerous opposite word pairings in many different languages with the same results. He came to the conclusion that the water seemed to correctly understand the essence of what it was shown. The feeling of the word seemed to be taken in by the water as information and it understood its meaning. The most powerful word combination was "love and gratitude." The crystal formation of water given this message was the most beautiful as it appeared as a fully blossoming flower. Emoto came to the conclusion that because the quality of water improves or deteriorates depending on the information given to it, the corollary for humans, who are made primarily of water, is to "take in" good information. He surmised that when we do, our mind and body can become healthier. Conversely, when we take in negative information, we can get sick.

When we consciously focus our attention and intention on the good things in life, we are actually creating health and balance for our physical body.

The implications of his work completely captivated me as an energy practitioner, as it supported my understanding that the energy currency for humans is what we think, say, believe, feel and do as we live our daily lives. When we consciously focus our attention and intention on the good things in life, we are actually creating health and balance for our physical body. Now when I drink a glass of water, I intentionally take a moment to bless it with love and gratitude for the health and wellness of my body and for the gift of life it represents.

When I conduct workshops, I demonstrate the nature of energy using a few practical exercises that allow participants to tune in and connect to their own energy as well as others. Then participants have firsthand experience of feeling and understanding that they are made of energy, and how they project and move this energy has implications not only for themselves but for others as well.

Let me share with you some exercises I use to teach this concept.

An exercise you can do right now that will connect you to your own energy begins as follows. First, sit in a chair with your feet flat on the floor and back straight and relaxed. Take a nice deep breath and begin to focus your attention and intention on feeling your own energy. Take a few more deep breaths to clear your mind and to focus on the task at hand.

Raise your hands in front you, shoulder width apart, with your palms facing each other. Take a breath and close your eyes. Now slowly move your palms towards each other and pay attention to any sensations or feelings that you may be sensing in the palms of your hand. Simply keep your awareness on your palms and ask, "Do I feel anything?" If not, continue to slowly move your palms towards each other. Everyone feels energy differently. You may feel a tingling in your palms or a temperature change. You may feel some pressure or resistance.

Once you feel "something," stop moving your palms and hold your hands still. Open your eyes to see how close your hands are to each other. Once you feel the energy and see your hands, begin to play with the energy by pushing it with your palms and then pulling the energy, much like you would do if you were pulling taffy or playing with an elastic band. You can use your hands to form the "energy" you are feeling into a ball and begin to shrink and expand it as you manipulate it.

Please note that not everyone will feel energy the first time they do this exercise. Keep practising until you do. Often limiting beliefs will interfere with the ability to connect to an idea that is outside your comfort zone. It is important that your mind is clear, and you are opening up to the idea that it is possible to feel your energy. Use your breath to clear your mind and relax. Just breathe and allow the energy to be present.

If you do this exercise with a partner, place your chairs opposite each other and face one another. Have your palms facing each other at shoulder height with a couple of feet between you. Close your eyes and take a nice deep breath. Set the intention to feel the energetic edge of your partner's energy field. Begin to move your hands toward your partner. The moment you feel a sensation in your palms, stop. Your partner may not feel it at the same time so communicate that you have stopped and each of you open your eyes. Your partner will now see where you are located, and they have reached the edge of your energy field that extends out from your physical body. If your partner continues to move their palms until they feel a sensation, you will see how far your energy field extends beyond your physical body as well.

This is a good example of why it is important that we are conscious of energy and that we all have a field of energy that surrounds us and connects us to others. As I mentioned earlier, this is referred to as our personal space. If you have ever felt uncomfortable when someone gets too close or enters your space without permission, this explains why.

The energy that surrounds us is a field and can be impacted easily by other people's energy if we are not paying attention. Notice the next time you are at a party or in a crowded place. Can you feel an energy shift when you are close to someone? Have you ever experienced walking into a room and knowing immediately something isn't quite right, as the energy feels tight and constrained? Or the opposite, you walk into a room and the energy feels upbeat and fun and it elevates you into a better state of being. The awareness of energy is an important cue for decision-making. If something doesn't feel good energetically, then you can decide to move away from it, avoid it or challenge it. If it feels good energetically, you can move toward it, participate in it and become it. The downside is if you are not paying attention, then you will be pulled into whatever field you are in and miss the opportunity to make a conscious decision of what you want to experience.

Here's another exercise that I conduct in my workshops to show how human energy can impact people, situations and experiences through personal thoughts, conscious or unconscious. This powerful experience shifts people's awareness into responsibility and care. Remember, our "thoughts" are energy and they are creative in nature.

First, I invite a participant to the front of the room. I ask the participant if they will step out of the room for a moment while we set up the experiment to prove that thoughts are energy and can impact the energy of a person they are projected onto. Once the participant is out of earshot, I instruct the audience that I will cue them with either a thumbs up or thumbs down to send thoughts of kindness or unkindness, respectively, to the participant. While they do this, I will muscle test the participant's energy using their extended arm as the calibrator of their energy.

Please note that muscle testing is a learned skill and there are numerous methods that can be used. *The Emotion Code* (Nelson, 2007) and *discoverhealing.com* are excellent resources for a detailed explanation and demonstration of a number of these methods.

For the purposes of this explanation, I used the method of applying pressure to the extended arm while thoughts are being sent from the audience. As I press down on the participant's arm, it will remain strong when the thoughts are kind, supportive and loving; conversely, the arm will weaken if the thoughts are unkind, unsupported and mean-spirited.

I invite the participant back into the room and instruct them to turn their back to the audience. The process of muscle testing is explained to the participant, and we begin with their arm being extended. I cue the audience to begin sending the thoughts I have instructed, and I then begin the muscle test. Within a few seconds of the thoughts being sent, the participant's energy is showing the effects of the thoughts. The most profound moment happens when the audience realizes that the loving thoughts they send, such as "you are smart, you are good looking, you are awesome, I love your hair, your eyes are beautiful, I love your style," have an impact on the participant's energy. Their arm is so strong that I would almost have to stand on it to get it to move. Conversely, when thoughts are unkind, such as "you are stupid, I hate your hair, you are ugly, you are too skinny/too fat, you look like a slob," the arm releases its power, and no matter how hard the participant tries mentally or manually to keep the arm strong, they cannot.

If you have never seen this exercise in action, please take note that it works. Even in the silence of your mind, your thoughts have the power to elevate or deflate another person's energy. Remember Mr. Emoto's work with water, knowing that your physical body is 70 per cent water. Understanding and knowing this means that taking personal responsibility for the thoughts you send out is important and necessary to create an energetic field to heal both yourself and the person you are projecting those thoughts onto. Remember, if your thoughts are energy and as the Law of Circle states, whatever you send out will return to you; negativity attracts more of itself, and more positive thoughts will attract more of it back to you. This knowledge can empower you to shift whatever isn't working in your life by paying attention to your own energy and ensuring that you are focusing on what it is you want to experience.

When you pay attention to your own energy and how you are feeling, you can manage and control how you react to people, experiences and situations that you may encounter in your daily life. When you ignore how you feel, you can be pulled into other people's energy and you will lose the ability to control your experience.

> ***When you pay attention to your own energy and how you are feeling, you can manage and control how you react to people, experiences and situations that you may encounter in your daily life.***

The breath is always the tool to use to create the pause when you notice the energy in your physical body or field is not serving you. It is also important to recognize that whatever energy you are projecting onto a person, situation or experience is having an impact on them, so be sure you are creating the energy that will serve you and not hurt you in the long run.

I always like to point out that our "words" also have great power, as demonstrated by Mr. Emoto's work. They can be used to be kind or not. The way you choose to express yourself (consciously or unconsciously) is an important key to living your best life. It becomes a choice or a decision you can make consciously to do better by short-circuiting the subconscious mind from running amok, such as not thinking before you speak. Shifting a mindset is about understanding that you have the power to make decisions that serve you and serve others in a much more loving and kind way.

Having a career in the field of energy healing requires that a practitioner understands the laws of energy. Many healing modalities offer healing through a process called "distance healing," which is made possible through the understanding of how energy works. The law simply states that energy will follow intention. A client can be connected energetically to a practitioner anywhere or anytime by setting up an appointment and agreeing to the process. This connection is always done with the client's permission coupled with the understanding of the work that will be completed. The conscious awareness through intention can create a healing space between the practitioner and the client.

This connection is possible because the practitioner acts as a proxy for the client. Proxy is when you give the practitioner permission to work in your field of energy to release or remove any blockages created by imbalances discovered in your energetic body. To go into proxy, the practitioner sets the intention to connect through the process of energy focusing. Remember, everything in the universe is energy, including the space that appears empty between objects. Although there is a great distance between the practitioner and you, the practitioner can focus their energy like a laser on you (with permission) and will connect almost like they have plugged an electrical cord into your field of energy from their own. This allows the practitioner to communicate using muscle testing (kinesiology) to ask your subconscious mind if there are any imbalances contributing to the issues you are experiencing.

The spiritual laws of energy forbid a practitioner from working in a person's energy field without their express permission. I always advise anyone that I work with that they have the power to control their energy through awareness and attention. Your energy field is yours to monitor and regulate. If you feel you are losing energy to something or someone, take a breath and invoke your power by closing off the energy moving into your field. With a simple command from your conscious mind, you state that any frequency that is not resonating at a level that is for your highest and greatest good it is not welcome.

> ***Your energy field is yours to monitor and regulate.***

I will offer two points of caution. Most people that work in the field of energy healing have noble intentions and a desire to support and guide people through a healing crisis. However, there are always those who do this work for profit and will offer outcomes that do not align with the intention of this work. Also, energy work is a complementary therapy that is designed to support the healing process. Therefore, if you are under a physician's care, this work does not replace the advice and treatments you might be receiving.

The information and intention in this part of the book invite you to shift or alter any mindset that might have you believing you are powerless to change your circumstances. The information provided in these last few pages offers you an alternate viewpoint or mindset. Ask yourself this question: if energy is the currency I carry to communicate within my physical body and also outside of my physical body, then is it not possible for me to be in charge of that energy when I am consciously aware and paying attention to how I feel? If I want to feel good, connected and in the flow of living my best life, then I need to pay attention to myself and how I feel so that I can shift into the energy that I want versus what I don't want. Now doesn't this sound simple? The answer is yes, but once again, it is not easy because you have to stay present and connected to do this work.

SPIRITUAL CONSCIOUSNESS

In David Hawkins' book *Power versus Force*, he presented a Map of Consciousness that was developed by the Institute of Advanced Spiritual Research. The map has influenced my understanding of human energy systems. As I have shared with you, there is strong evidence to suggest we are not alone in the universe and there is a higher power guiding us into consciousness to know our true nature, value and purpose on the planet.

The Map of Consciousness shows the link between a person's perception of this higher power and their life view or experience. The conclusion is the less connected you are to this higher power, the more difficult your life will be. Remember that your connection to this higher power is not through your mind; it is through the energy of your heart. This can be validated by how we feel when we are lost in the busyness of our minds versus when we are connected to the expansive energy of our heart.

The separation from your heart creates a feeling of isolation, loneliness or abandonment from self and others. This separation can fuel many of the lower emotional energies that will cause you to feel stuck and stagnant in life. When you begin to contemplate and connect and have an experience with this higher power (similar to mine in the hospital), it is easier to accept that you are not alone. Once connected to this belief, it can create all kinds of openings for your life force energy to take root and grow.

Having studied human consciousness for several years, I began to see how powerful my consciousness and energy output was in creating balance and harmony not only in my own physical body but also in all areas of my life.

The interconnectedness of all energy makes me feel personally responsible on a daily basis for my own energy. Whatever energy is sent out from a person's field of energy will connect with the collective consciousness that will influence the energy everywhere on the planet. This then begs the following question. Is it possible that when we live unconsciously, feeling like victims of circumstance, these fear-based energies are polluting our atmosphere and creating discordant and negative energy around the planet? You have probably heard about the butterfly effect: when a butterfly flaps its wings in one part of the world, it can change the weather in another part of the world as the energy it initially created picks up momentum as it gathers similar energy on its path across land and water. That is how our energy works with the energy that surrounds us.

The separation from your heart creates a feeling of isolation, loneliness or abandonment from self and others.

When you think of our planet now and the need for our attention to heal it, it mirrors what is required within the physical body. The planet needs clean water and food supplies to sustain life, as we do. The air we breathe is essential for life, and so we must care for the planet, the trees and all of nature to ensure that we will have the air we need to continue living. If we see ourselves as separate and cut off from this responsibility, then we are part of the problem rather than part of the solution.

Waking up to the truth that you are "energy" and a spiritual being residing in a physical body helps to put individual responsibilities into perspective. Taking responsibility by being "self-ish" through consciousness, care and love gives you the opportunity to see the power of your decisions to live in harmony and balance.

Focusing your attention and intention inward to heal and strengthen the connection to the "self" ultimately creates the opportunity to live your best life while at the same time supporting others and the planet. The reminder is that you can only give energetically what you have, so if your energy is full of all the emotional energies that keep you conscious and in harmony with the good things in life, you are essentially healing self and the planet as a whole.

Focusing your attention and intention inward to heal and strengthen the connection to the "self" ultimately creates the opportunity to live your best life while at the same time supporting others and the planet.

Take a breath. This is so amazing. Each one of us can be a co-creator of our experience by tapping into the most powerful energy source on the planet. This power source is located in the middle of your chest, my chest and everyone else's. The heart is the energy centre of the human body. When you connect to the "collective" consciousness through your heart energy, you have the power and control to change difficult situations into less difficult ones.

The most profound work I have done as an energy practitioner is using the Emotion and Body Code protocols to release what is called a heart wall. In his book *The Emotion Code*, Bradley Nelson explains the discovery and removal of the heart wall in detail.

Briefly, the heart wall is made of emotional energies and traumas of the past. The theory is that these emotional energies create a barrier to protect the part of us that holds the blueprint or truth of who we are. The truth is based on a belief that all of humanity was created (the gift of life) from a Divine spark of pure energy that was perfect, whole and complete. Let's call this energy "love." This spark is within each of us and resides in the area of our hearts. When this spark is activated, it feels expansive and amazingly good. If you have practised the heart-based breathing process I shared with you, you will have firsthand experience of this feeling.

However, because of all the "things" that have been said and done to us over our lifetime, these emotional traumas have blocked our ability to "feel" this connection to our heart and also to the good things in life. The theory is that the heart wall, acting as a protective barrier, will remain intact until you are ready to enter into the healing process. As the heart wall releases the flow of energy into and out of the heart, the heart begins allowing you to reclaim your personal power through the frequencies of "love" for self and others. Once reconnected to your heart energy, all the gifts, passions and talents you carry can be activated so that you can live your best life.

For the purpose of this book, I want to emphasize that your disconnection from the energy of your heart is significant. It reduces your ability to shift your mindsets and to connect to your spirit or life force energy as it was intended to flow and function. The energy of the heart is what connects you to the field of energy that surrounds you and to the light side of your emotional being. Through the release of your heart wall, you are able to connect with the part of yourself that carries the blueprints of your gifts and passions. When the heart is open to give and receive energy, it becomes the conduit for all good things to enter your life that will inspire you to create the life that you thought you could only dream about.

Remember how you breathe into your heart and you activate feelings of gratitude and appreciation? This is how you can begin to reconnect with your heart energy. Removal of trapped emotions and memories is hugely beneficial. A practitioner can assist you in this process or you can begin now by simply connecting with your breath and your intention to release the "shadow emotions" that are keeping you stuck and stalled in your life.

Do you feel the energy in your chest expanding when you breathe into your heart and activate appreciation and gratitude? I know I do.

When our heart energy is open and expanding, we are connecting to the energy field or collective consciousness in a way that will support all areas of our life and those of others who are sending out the same signal. Think about the momentum of "love" energy in your life and on the planet if everyone focused their intention and attention on healing and living their best life. Remember that self-awareness, care and love are the basis for this process to gain momentum and power to ignite the flame of your passions.

The bigger message here is that if each one of us becomes self-conscious enough to be aware of our energy "currencies" (beliefs, thoughts, words, feelings and actions), then we will be empowered to create the experiences we want versus the ones we do not want. This takes practice, commitment, faith, trust and most of all surrender.

> ***Judgment of others is a huge shadow that many of us would do well to practise less of.***

Remember I said earlier that I wanted to figure out where the feeling of bliss came from when I was in the hospital with my husband? I realize now that the feeling was created through the act of surrender. This act meant I gave over my will or my want to whatever was meant to happen for the greatest good of my husband. When I accepted that I had done everything I could, I had to trust that whatever was meant to happen would, and I would be okay.

It is the same when you begin to do this work for yourself. If you do the work to know yourself and move your energy by opening up your heart and connecting to the possibilities that exist for you, the "how" of it will be taken care of. Release control of how it unfolds; have faith, trust and surrender as you continue to move towards your passion and purpose. Don't stop the flow and wait—you must participate. Be inspired to watch as your life takes on a whole new direction because you are doing the work, and the universe will support the flow of your conscious intention to create the life of your dreams.

I need to explain the emotional energy of judgment now because some readers may be thinking, "Okay, this is way deeper into the healing process than I am willing to go." I am asking you to suspend judgment and to open your mind for a few more paragraphs.

Judgment of others is a huge shadow that many of us would do well to practise less of. Through the process of self-awareness and the laws of energy, I have learned that judgment is more about the person judging than the person being judged. Having an opinion that differs from another is normal and expected as we are all unique in our perspectives. However, when we try to influence others with power over energy and force, we have crossed the line into making someone else wrong in order for us to be right. We only have to look at the larger conflicts in the world to know that this is a truth.

Celebrating our differences through discernment and loved-based energies creates fields of energy within the collective web such as compassion, co-operation, caring, conciliation and open communication versus the fear-based energies that take us into shadow and discordant outcomes.

Having explained the difference between judgment and discernment, I would offer to those who feel some opposition to my ideas to just hold the space and continue to read until the end. I am not asking for everyone to agree, but simply to take the time to contemplate the possibility.

The pursuit to understand consciousness and the conditions required to get there has led me and continues to lead me on a path of connection to data and information through books, courses and people who serve to ground me in the mindset that "connected we stand and divided we fall." We are not alone.

The shift in my mindset allows me to experience more deeply and more often the moments of bliss that inspired me in the beginning of my journey to discover my purpose and passion to live my best life. This is something you will need to decide for yourself. What are your beliefs around religion and spirituality?

It would be a disservice not to share with you the multitude of authors, coaches and courses I have taken to build my arsenal of data and information. This information became the knowledge I used to do the work and create my healing practice. The experience of using my skills and sharing them with others has allowed me to gain the wisdom I have now to share with others seeking to move from a difficult situation to a less difficult one.

You will find at the back of the book courses, coaches and books that were influential in creating the content of this book. The purpose of this information is to provide some resources that you can also tap into. These resources will give you a broader and deeper dive into the material I have tried to simplify for you in this book.

FOUNDATIONAL REQUIREMENTS FOR HEALTH

Based on my personal experience and knowledge and through the program of self-awareness, care and love, I developed a perspective on how I viewed the body's health and well-being. I came up with four criteria that I call the Foundational Requirements for Health.

Similar to the foundation of a house, which supports and balances the structure, the physical body needs a strong foundation to do the same. The four pillars that support the body's foundation are: (1) a good night's sleep; (2) good, clean, organic (if possible) food and water; (3) movement/ mobility/exercise; and (4) a strong mental/emotional/spiritual life.

The four pillars that support the body's foundation are: (1) a good night's sleep; (2) good, clean, organic (if possible) food and water; (3) movement/ mobility/ exercise; and (4) a strong mental/ emotional/spiritual life.

I focus my practice on the fourth pillar; however, the other three are as important and necessary to heal and balance your life. My study into human energy systems included training and certification in several hands-on-healing modalities. Reflexology, acupressure, reiki, therapeutic touch and integrated energy therapy were a few that I practised. Each modality worked with the human energy field, and I, as the practitioner, would move into the field of the client with the intention of moving their energy to relax, calm, regulate and circulate any stagnant energy that might be contributing to issues and concerns in their physical body.

The outcome in most cases was always a "temporary" release of pain and discomfort for the client. Most clients would experience an improvement in their issue after one session. However, over time the issue would tend to resurface, their energy would become imbalanced and once again their overall well-being declined. There appeared to be other underlying issues that we were missing that continued to trigger the issue for the client. Hence, the clients experienced a temporary relief from their discomfort.

To give you an idea of how this works, I will explain reflexology. The energy of the body has been studied for over 5,000 years in Eastern cultures. As a result, the flow of energy has been mapped out and located within the physical body. Acupuncture is a perfect example of when and how this map of energy is used to heal the body. There are essentially seven or eight vortexes of energy that run along the length of the spinal cord into the head or crown of the body. These energy vortexes have specific energy signatures and purposes. Along with these energy vortices, there are 12 lines or meridians of energy that run from our extremities, either up or down the length of the human body, head to toe, to fingers. These energy meridians run in, through and around all structures, tissues, organs, glands and other parts of the human anatomy. Carolyn Myss's book *Spirit of the Anatomy* is an excellent resource for understanding how they work. Another excellent reference book is Donna Eden's book *Energy Medicine*.

In reflexology, the energy meridians and spinal energy vortexes are located on the head, hands and feet. The practitioner, using massage and manipulation techniques, will set the intention to move any stagnant energy that may be contributing to physical issues the client may be suffering with. Reflexology has been proven to promote pain relief, relaxation and calmness in the body as the hands-on technique creates connection and flow to areas of the body that may have been congested or blocked.

Reflexology is also used in hospitals to help promote the healing process. Research has shown that there is a qualitative improvement in recovery in patients who receive reflexology treatments before and after surgical procedures versus those that don't. A patient who is calm and relaxed going into a procedure is more likely to come out of it stronger, and the body's natural healing ability will be initiated as the energy is open and flowing.

You many have noticed that I said that in most cases "temporary" release of pain and discomfort could be initiated in the hands-on treatment modalities I had listed. My curiosity got the best me and I wanted to understand why the treatments only lasted for a temporary period of time. If you remember from my own health crisis that I shared with you, I worked with my reflexology teachers who provided me with treatments every few days to help me rebuild my energy reserves. I would feel amazing after each treatment. However, within a few days my energy would be tanked again, and we would have to start over.

This cycle was repeated for several weeks. Finally, as I began to get a handle on other areas of my life, my health and energy began to improve and replenish. Importantly, I had to take responsibility for the healing process. It was up to me to notice what I was feeling and make decisions to support my self-care. This included diet, exercise, lots of sleep and dealing with my emotional "fears." My spiritual coach at that time saved me from my "self."

Over a few years of researching and studying the energy systems at a deeper level, I was introduced to the work of Bradley Nelson, author of *The Emotion Code* and creator of the Body Code System. The premise of *The Emotion Code* is that emotional energies can become trapped in the energy systems of the human body. When they do, they can create a disruption of the energy flow in whatever part of the body they are stored, leading to possible "issues in your tissues." The intention of releasing these stored emotions/memories is to assist the client to open up the energy flow in their body systems to promote healing. The simple awareness of what was "causing" or "contributing" to the symptoms they were experiencing allowed the client to feel more connected to their bodies.

Nelson's work fascinated me, so in 2009 and 2012, respectively, I certified and trained to become an Emotion Code and Body Code Practitioner. I soon shifted my practice from hands-on healing modalities to the emotional release of energy using the new tools I had acquired, coupled with my Psych-K training.

Briefly, Psych-K (Williams, 2004) is an energy modality that focuses on identifying beliefs by muscle testing specific points of the body for weakness and strength. Beliefs, as I discussed in Chapter 2, are usually the anchor for emotional traumas and for creating repeat patterns or habits of behaviour. The beliefs are stored in the "hard drive" of the subconscious mind and are accessed when the belief is triggered. By using Emotion and Body Code (Nelson, 2007) and Psych-K (Williams, 2004) as my main "energy" tools, I was able to provide a specialized treatment plan for my clients.

Many of my clients came to me because they had exhausted medical intervention and were now in a state of being stuck in their life with physical, mental/emotional or spiritual issues. They found me either on the practitioner website of Healer's Library, now known as *discoverhealing.com*, or as a referral/contact through my website *footprintshome.org*.

The problem with most of my clients was that whatever pain they experienced or illness they had, they could not get to its source. Many felt disconnected and confused about what to do and where to go to get the help they needed. Trying something outside the box seemed to be better than nothing.

> ***Your health is directly related to how energy moves through your body. Remember, it is called "life-force energy."***

Everything that I have shared with you so far, coupled with your ability to learn and practise, will assist you in working towards preventive measures in your goal for health and balance. If you are feeling stuck or stagnant in your life, this information can assist you to get your energy moving. The breath is key, as I have emphasized. However, this is not a job that can be done alone. My healing journey and those I have learned from all went through their own healing crisis and reached out for support and guidance throughout the process of getting better. It was only when they had gained mastery of their healing that they had the ability to share the knowledge and wisdom to guide those who follow.

Please understand that healing is personal for everyone. Doing the work I have outlined, coupled with some strategies to develop the skill sets to stay conscious, is only one pillar of your foundation. Remember, the other three pillars need your attention and focus. As you develop self-awareness and self-love, I believe that many of your issues will begin to balance. You may find you take the time to prepare healthier meals, drink that extra eight ounces of water or go to the gym because you have more energy and desire to live your best life.

The willingness to do the work, to accept responsibility for outcomes and to constantly connect with your power centre (your heart) are essential and necessary to keep the process moving and clearing. Your health is directly related to how energy moves through your body. Remember, it is called "life-force energy."

I will never forget an episode of Oprah. In 2007 she was interviewing a gentleman by the name of John Diaz, who had survived an airplane crash. His experience was horrifying. He told Oprah the following story. In the chaos of a burning plane with people strapped in their seats and most unable to escape, he witnessed an astonishing sight in his last moment before exiting the plane. He saw energy in the form of light—he referred to it as an aura—lifting from the bodies of those who had died. What struck him as he contemplated what he saw was that some of the light coming from the passengers was bright and expansive whereas other people's aura was small and congested.

Remember that energy that is created cannot be destroyed.

Having been given a second chance at life, Diaz told Oprah what he learned from the experience. He wanted to live a bigger life in service to others. He shared with Oprah that from his experience, he had become "more empathetic" and in so doing was "increasing his light." He said when his time came to crossover from this life to the next, he wanted to shine bright and expansive, demonstrating he had not wasted his time and energy on things of little importance in this life. He wanted to have made a difference.

This powerful story validated for me that our physical bodies do die, but the "life force energy" that flows through us appears not to. Through the visual experience of this man, his story demonstrated that energy leaves our body at the time of our death. Could this energy be our life force/spirit, our soul? Think about this for a moment. Remember that energy that is created cannot be destroyed.

Pause right now and take a breath. Breathe this knowledge into your heart and allow yourself to feel the expansive nature of your heart as it opens up to this perspective or idea. If our life force energy, a.k.a.

spirit, can never be destroyed, does that not mean that our "spirit" is eternal? This is heady stuff.

Many books have been written on near-death experiences and communication with our deceased loved ones; they have often been brushed off by the skeptics as mere magical thinking. Researching, studying and witnessing the amazing experiences of people like John Diaz has inspired me to focus my attention and work in the realm of energy and healing. I understand more deeply the power I have to control my life experiences and energy. This knowledge is what makes me want to get up in the morning with the desire to live my best life.

The idea that energy is created and cannot be destroyed is inspiring. It takes away the fear of death and activates a greater desire to live a life of conscious awareness and presence. This becomes the impulse to focus and direct your vision towards living your best life, just like the man on the Oprah show.

Paying attention and controlling your own energy lets you take charge of your life and the experiences that you want to have. When you seek to fix things from outside sources without doing the inner work first, many of the issues that you experience will repeat in patterns or become old habits only to return to be experienced again. The reason is simply that you can't fix what you don't acknowledge, and what you don't acknowledge can't be fixed. If you have watched the Dr. Phil show, you will have seen the truth of this statement play out in real-life dramas. This is where reality television may have a bigger message if you are paying attention. Many of the dramas that unfold on his show illustrate how behaviours and patterns created cannot be fixed until the people involved take personal responsibility and stop blaming others.

Paying attention and controlling your own energy lets you take charge of your life and the experiences that you want to have.

Taking responsibility does not mean the burden of your awareness needs to be carried alone. The foundational structure of your health depends on you paying attention to the structural integrity of each of the pillars that hold you in balance. When you are out of alignment and your structural integrity is compromised, you have choices to make. You can either ignore it or acknowledge it through conscious awareness. Taking responsibility is the impetus for change.

Let me share a story with you to illustrate the point I am making.

In 2009, I had recently become a certified Emotion Code Practitioner. A new client had reached out through a referral from his wife. He asked if he could come for a session, as he was experiencing "level eight pain" (with 10 being the most intense) in his neck and left shoulder and had exhausted everything medically, other than surgery, to alleviate the pain.

I explained to him that the Emotion Code is a technique that works to identify and release trapped emotional energies that may be creating the issues in his physical structure. I went on to explain that emotions are energy, and when they nest in the physical body, they can block, constrict, restrict or congest the flow of energy to other body systems, creating pain and discomfort. Our work together would involve identifying the trapped emotions, if any, and then through this awareness, release the emotion from his physical body and energy field. The release is made possible through the intention and conscious awareness of the client. The expectation is that once the emotional energy is released, the flow of energy to the affected area would open up and allow the healing process to begin. Our goal was for him to be pain-free.

> ***Taking responsibility is the impetus for change.***

When the client came to see me, we did a brief history of his injury to his neck. He demonstrated the limitation of his mobility. He could only turn his head in one direction without pain. His range of motion was deficient, and his level of pain registered at seven to eight. He said the mornings were the worst; when he woke up, it would take him awhile to warm up the muscles to lift his head and get out of bed with as little pain as possible.

He had been a football player in high school and through his university years. He had several injuries, including a broken collarbone and other injuries to his neck and shoulder. He had done all types of bodywork, including massage therapy, physiotherapy and chiropractic. He came to me because the next option was to operate on his neck to fuse the spine, something he did not want to have done.

Once he had shared his situation, I asked him if he was willing to work with emotional energies to see if there was an underlying issue that he was holding onto that was contributing to the pain in his neck and shoulder.

He agreed, and with his permission, I began the process of entering his field of energy using muscle testing as my entry point. To clarify the process again, muscle testing uses kinesiology to determine the openness of the body to release energy. When you muscle test someone's energy, you are actually accessing their subconscious mind to make specific statements that only have yes or no answers. For example, if I were to be muscle tested, the practitioner would state "My name is Sharon" while pressing down gently on my arm. If the arm remains strong, the answer is yes; if the arm weakens, it is not a true statement.

Please note, the practitioner first muscle tests their own energy to ensure that they are working in the field of their client's energy and not their own. Muscle testing is a skill anyone can learn and become proficient at. However, like any new skill, conscious awareness and practice are essential, followed by repetition, repetition, repetition, until the skill is learned and becomes automatic.

Once I was in the client's energy field and he was relaxed and open, we began asking the following questions: Do I have a trapped emotional energy that is contributing to the pain I am experiencing in my neck and shoulder? The answer was yes. Using the Emotion Code Table of Emotions from *The Emotion Code* (Nelson, 2007), I was able to muscle test and uncover the emotions that were the underlying contributors to his pain.

For each emotion I discovered, the process involved uncovering bits and pieces of information to expose a memory that the client might remember of a person, event or situation that created the emotional trauma that was stored. To do this, I would muscle test and ask at what age did he trap this emotional energy, and as I would go through the timeline of his life, the age would be revealed. When he had that information, we could continue asking questions such as "did this emotional event involve a person or a place?" Each question would uncover more information until the client remembered the trigger moment.

Please note that it is not essential for the trigger moment to be identified in the release process. The subconscious mind can hold onto the memory while releasing the emotion; the result is the same. Often clients will share that they remember and still do "feel" the emotion we revealed, but they never understood where it came from. Learning that they trapped it as a young child gives them permission to suspend self-judgment and accept that they can now give themselves permission to let it go.

Getting back to my client story, during our session the first emotion we released was the emotional energy of "unworthy." This emotional energy is defined in Bradley Nelson's Definition of Emotions Chart (Nelson, 2007) as "not good enough; beneath the dignity of; not commendable or credible; undeserving; not valuable or suitable; unbecoming." When my client connected with the frequency, I watched his shoulders slump, his head drop and tears filled his eyes. As we held the space together, I asked him if he wanted to move on to see at what age he trapped this emotion. He looked up at me and said there was no need. "This is about my dad. I have never felt good enough in his eyes. He was always so critical of me and nothing I ever did was good enough for him. I have spent my lifetime trying to prove to him my worthiness, and he died before I accomplished this. I push myself beyond my limits, not only in sport but all areas of my life trying to prove that I can." As he sat and let this emotion wash over him, the tears came and went, and gradually we were able to continue.

At this point in the session, I asked if he was willing to release the emotion along with the memory attached to it. I explained to him that his conscious awareness of this long-standing belief—that he was not good enough—could now be released from his subconscious "programming," much like a file is deleted on a computer hard drive. The coaching I offered was that if he consciously released the emotion of unworthy from the hard drive of his mind, he could also consciously write a new program called "I am worthy."

Using the intention of releasing the "unworthy" energy, we focused on his breath and created the energy flow in his body to move unworthy from his neck and shoulders. We visualized the energy being released into the field surrounding him to be transmuted into love and light. Using the Psych-K protocol of Energy Focusing (Williams, 2004), we replaced the released energy with a new frequency called "I am worthy of all the best that love and life have to offer." We stayed in this energy until he felt a shift.

When I muscled tested "I am unworthy," his arm weakened. This validated we had released the emotion and it was not true. I muscle tested "I am worthy," and his arm was like a brick wall. It could not be moved. That was a resounding yes. I asked him to take a moment and slowly move his neck back and forth, and to both our amazement, his range of motion had improved almost 100 per cent. He said the pain level had dropped from the seven to eight to a level two to three.

The reason we were both amazed was because of how quickly the energy had regulated to shift his pain and mobility. We continued the session through another two emotional releases, and my client left feeling more comfortable and in control of his body and spirit. I wish I could tell you if this client is sustaining these releases to this day, but he did not return after our initial session. However, I did receive a few emails following that session, thanking me for my guidance and support and saying he did not go through with the surgery on his neck. He said he was managing the pain through his awareness and care. He said he was also working on learning how to forgive the past so he could live more fully in the present. As a practitioner, I couldn't have been happier with the immediate results. However, as a coach I would have loved to participate in more sessions to see the transformative value of this client's attention to his "self" and his care.

The important message in this example is that our subconscious mind takes our experiences and creates "programming" around what we perceive to be true and then develops a belief to validate that perception. In the example above, my client perceived that in his father's eyes he never measured up to his expectations. He constantly felt his father judged him, and he interpreted and internalized that judgment as a feeling of not good enough that became the belief of unworthy. As a result, he became an overachiever to prove his worth, and his emotional pain lodged in his neck as if he were carrying the weight of the world on his shoulders.

Understanding that your perceptions are only real to you is critically important. They do not apply to anyone else. Therefore, it is important to recognize that what you believe to be true will not be true for someone else. I have come to understand that whatever my client's father was projecting on his son was never about his son, it was about him, the father. Because the father wasn't equipped with the knowledge to do his own healing work, his pain became a way to blame and project what he lacked onto his son. This is how family history repeats itself generationally until someone figures out the pattern and changes it.

> ***Understanding that your perceptions are only real to you is critically important. They do not apply to anyone else.***

This is true for so many of us. We must learn to pay attention to the critical voice in our head, whether you think it is father, mother, boss, friend, sibling or someone else, because the truth is the voice is not them, it is you. The voice is the subconscious perception of what you believe about yourself. When you hear the voice and you observe it through conscious awareness, use your breath and allow it to speak. Then you gain control of the next decision you make. Do you believe the voice, or do you believe in yourself?

I constantly tell my clients that someone else's bad behaviour is never about them, it is always about the person who is projecting and blaming something or someone else for the issues in their life. If you can simply take a breath, hold the space, create a pause and let the person's projection or bad behaviour move through you, rather than taking it in as a truth, it will go a long way to help in your healing process.

A friend once said to me that it is none of your business what someone else thinks about you. Their thoughts have more to do with them than about you, unless you choose to believe them. This was a valuable lesson. I realized I had spent so much of my life caring about what others thought about me and never questioned myself as to whether what they said was true or not.

Think about this. Do you have any memories of someone saying something to you that really hurt your feelings and then afterwards you began to change your behaviour because you believed them? Let me give you a generalized example of what I am asking.

Think about a young child just learning a new skill at school. They are struggling with the task and can't quite grasp how to do it. The teacher, out of frustration and anger, has reached the end of their rope and says to the child, "What are you, stupid?" The child hears the word stupid, connects it to the inability to learn the task and decides that he must be stupid if he can't figure it out.

The teacher probably didn't mean to say those words, but it was a bad day and they were tired. The boy, however, takes it in and whenever he is learning a new task and struggles, the program "I am stupid" is triggered and he gives up. Remember the discussion about the subconscious mind in Chapter Two. The subconscious mind takes your beliefs, thoughts, words, feelings and actions literally, so it will program "I am stupid" to be triggered every time this child, teenager and eventually adult responds to failures and challenges in his life. I can't do this because "I am stupid." This creates the belief that you are a failure, nothing ever works out in your life, you can't keep a job or a relationship, and you are not good enough to be happy and successful.

> ***When someone is projecting or blaming you for something, it is in all likelihood more about them than you, but how you respond to them is all about you.***

This is how emotional trauma from the past can wreak havoc with the present if we don't stay present with what we are feeling. This is when it is essential that you "take a breath," pause and ask yourself, "Do I believe their perception of me or do I believe in me?" I can't tell you how many times I have said to someone who has judged me that I appreciate their perspective, but it really is none of my business what they think of me. When someone is projecting or blaming you for something, it is in all likelihood more about them than you, but how you respond to them is all about you.

Going back to the client who believed that his father perceived him as unworthy, I asked him if he was willing to recreate the memory of his father during our session by saying to himself what he needed to hear from his father. To recreate the memory, he imagined his father telling him how proud he was of him and all he had accomplished. As my client did this, he used heart-based breathing to allow his energy to shift out of his head and into his heart, where he felt the love that he had felt for his father. It was a transformational moment for him, and I could see his energy lift and open as he looked at me and smiled.

I told him that the only thing that I believed he was missing in his current life was what he wasn't giving himself, which was the self-worth that would help him to heal and forgive himself and his father for what he had believed to be true. Changing his mindset and belief about himself was the healing energy he needed to move through this challenge.

The mechanism to control balance in the body is through your "conscious" mind and your attention to what you are experiencing.

This client's story demonstrated that our human energy system, coupled with the other three pillars of health and balance, has the innate ability to heal our physical body. We were all born with this internal mechanism to self-heal as it is part of the body's intelligence. You just have to watch a wound heal on your body to know this to be true. A labourer who begins his career will suffer from blisters and wounds to the hand until calluses develop over time to protect him. The body knows what to do and when to do it.

The body systems must be open and communicating through the energy network to sustain and maintain the health and balance of the physical body. When your physical body is out of balance, your mind, body and spirit will allow your life force energy to survive and thrive. One health pillar cannot be ignored for another.

Individual responsibility is necessary and essential for balance to be attainable within your body systems. The air you breathe, the food and water you ingest, the sleep you get, movement, and your mental/emotional/spiritual self all need to be regulated, calibrated and nurtured to create the health that you want. You are the only one who can make these decisions for yourself. Nothing outside of you can do it.

When you understand that the ability to survive and thrive is built into the design of the human energy systems, it gives you the power to make the decisions necessary to regulate your health and well-being. Remembering that the human energy systems are driven subconsciously by the "innate" programming within the "hard drive" of our mind will free you to focus on the other priorities in your life.

This means that the mechanism to control balance in the body is through your "conscious" mind and your attention to what you are experiencing. If you are not paying attention and you are unconscious and just going through the motions of living, you have given your power away and will experience whatever your subconscious mind picks up through your senses without screening it for truth.

This is the key to unlock the door so you can step into the field of living your best life. Pay attention and stay present, use your breath to move you out of the sympathetic nervous system and into the parasympathetic, where all healing is possible.

TAKE A BREATH! I know many of the concepts in this book have been repeated numerous times. I am doing this purposefully. Everything that I am sharing with you is interconnected and flowing constantly. It is important that you are reminded about consciousness, decision-making and self-care so that you recognize that the power you possess to live your best life is within you—it is NOT outside of you. Your understanding of the human energy system and its connection to your physical body is critically important to the process of shifting and changing your life in the direction of what you want and what is possible when you are moving towards it with passion and purpose.

> ***The power you possess to live your best life is within you—it is NOT outside of you.***

This can only be done when you take a breath, stay present and focus on what you want to experience versus what you don't. Your health can be a personal messenger to let you know where your energy is moving or not. Physical pain is telling you to pause, reflect and focus your intention and attention on you and what to do next to shift and change the experience. This is where you make the decisions to seek guidance and support from those you feel connected to and trust in the process of discovering the contributors or causes to that pain. The beauty is that you get to make these decisions when you are connected and loving yourself enough to do the work necessary to find the answers.

The next topic is acceptance and resistance. These two energies are important in supporting the information that I have just shared with you.

TAKE A BREATH, clear your mind and open up to this information as it will assist you in the healing process and will also give you the power you need to move from your current situation to one that might make you feel better.

ACCEPTANCE VERSUS RESISTANCE

The energy of acceptance has multiple meanings. The following quote has stood out for me and guided me in transforming my life:

"Acceptance doesn't mean resignation; it means understanding that something is what it is and there's got to be a way through it."
~ Michael J. Fox

Acceptance coupled with taking responsibility for your current circumstances is a powerful duo of energies to help shift your life from something that is difficult to something that is less difficult. If you are someone who is stuck or stalled in life, begin by assessing your situation for what it is and then deciding what to do next to get you moving forward or through it. The decision to do something is you accepting responsibility for whatever outcome follows if you decide to move.

"Nothing happens until something moves."
~ Albert Einstein

When resistance shows up, it is an indicator that you are not accepting something. You will begin to feel like your wheels are spinning or you are caught in a never-ending circle of same old, same old. The saying "what you resist persists" is a perfect representation of what you have learned about the Law of the Circle and the frequency of emotional energies. Resistance is the shadow side of acceptance. In resistance, we are holding back energy, which will accumulate and cause blockage and constriction in the flow of energy or, in the case of your physical body, life force energy.

I will give you an example of a client of mine who was struggling with her living accommodations. She had recently been divorced and in the settlement was given a substantial amount of money to provide for herself and her son. She was currently living in a smaller space that was comfortable, but it was not what she wanted. She had a vision in her head of the house she wanted and its general location. However, she was stuck in her current living conditions and unable to find the place she most wanted. She shared that she was living out of boxes and was going through the motions of living in this space.

I listened carefully to her description of her current home and asked her to tell me more about the physical look and flow of her space. She began to describe it in more detail. She said it actually had really nice bones in that the layout was intimate and cosy. The windows were large and allowed lots of light in, and despite its size, it had potential. I asked her if she would be willing to do an experiment with me over the next few weeks. She agreed and we set up the following conditions.

She had to unpack her boxes and put her things away. I told her it was important for her to decorate and set up her place the way she would in her dream home, understanding that her current home was it. "It is what it is," I told her.

After a few days, I got an email in which she shared how she had discovered through her unpacking her favourite wine glasses and flower vase that she had forgotten she had. She said she went out and bought her favourite wine and some flowers to fill the vase. She said that as she sat at her dining table enjoying her wine and beautiful centrepiece, a feeling of contentment flowed through her. In her last comment, she said, "You know, this place is really comfortable, and I am beginning to feel like I am at home."

Our next session was three weeks later. In that time frame, she had completely settled into her little space and said that every time she walked in the door, she fell in love with it a bit more. She said although it would not be her forever space, for now it really suited her needs, and all of her things fit in and surrounded her to make it feel like home.

I asked her if she was still looking for any new real estate. She said that she hadn't been paying attention as she had been busy working on settling into her current place, but she felt she would get back to it soon. I suggested that she continue our experiment and that she begin to set the intention energetically through her vision of her dream home to begin the process of looking again. She agreed and thought that there was no better time than the present.

Within a week of our session, I get a phone call from this client and she was beyond excited. She said,

> *"Sharon, you are never going to believe what happened. I decided to drive through my dream neighbourhood, and when I reached the corner of my favourite street, there was a real estate agent putting up a sign on a property I had been admiring for years. I couldn't believe it, so I parked in front of the house and went to talk to the agent. After a brief discussion about the house, I told her I was very interested in it and would like to make an appointment to do a walk through. She told me the homeowner was away and had given the okay to start showing the house, so she asked me if I wanted to see it now as she was available. I walked through it and it is everything I have been dreaming about, floor plan, yard, location, cost, everything. It is like I manifested it myself. Needless to say, I started the ball rolling and will be putting an offer in today."*

This is not a coincidence or accident. This client who had been stuck and stalled in an area of her life had been resisting making her home a home because she thought that there was something better for her out there. That was true, but meanwhile another issue was playing out in her life that needed her attention: her inability to accept her current situation for what it was. She blocked her life force energy from creating a field of energy for what she wanted because the universe listened directly and literally took her unconscious desire to heart and helped to manifest only what she wanted, which was wanting her dream home not having it.

This is a difficult concept to take in. I was able to make sense of it through my own practice and experience of accepting "what is" before trying to create what "I want." In his book *Conversation with God*, Neale Donald Walsch said when we set up a "want" energy in our life, it is creating the field of "want" not a field of "have." How I interpreted this concept in relation to healing was in understanding the laws of energy.

The laws are specific: you cannot give what you do not have, and you cannot have what you cannot give. Said in another way, this means that your power resides in accepting where and what you have now and understanding that to change it you must do the work to get your energy moving in the direction you want to go. The energy of accepting what is—without judgment of it being good or bad—allows you to visualize and dream about what comes next.

The energy of accepting what is—without judgment of it being good or bad—allows you to visualize and dream about what comes next.

In my client's experiment, we tested this: if she stopped "wanting" her dream home through the process of accepting that her current living arrangement was home, then the ability to create a new field of energy for her next home would be possible. I hope you are going "wow" right now because that is exactly what I did when she shared this with me. To finish the story, a week later my client was the proud owner of her dream home, whereas five weeks earlier she was in the energy of wanting it.

This particular experiment and its result became a huge tool for me as a practitioner, because I now had firsthand experience witnessing the power of our life force energy to co-create our life experience. This example also answered the question I had asked about why my husband healed from his illness whereas someone else might not have been as fortunate. The answer to the question of "why" he did heal was because he did; however, my question was what was different about his healing from someone else's? The answer was he didn't put up any resistance to the healing process. Although he admits that fear showed up at times to take him down a dark tunnel, he consistently moved it aside as he focused on his healing. He accepted he was sick, but he also accepted that he could heal by doing all the things that his medical support team asked of him. He believed he would heal and he did. He had a goal and worked with that goal in mind at all times. I cannot say with certainty that is what happened. However, my faith, trust and surrender to the unseen forces allowed me to watch with amazement the strength of the human spirit as it moved through my husband.

I worked with this concept with numerous clients. The process takes longer with some more than others. The reason is as unique as each of the people with whom I have worked. It is so much easier to resist change than it is to accept change. We all have a path, and everything will always be perfectly timed for our healing and our transition to whatever awaits us. This is about having faith in the process and trusting yourself to do your work and surrendering outcome as everything will fall in to place as it is meant to. The universe always takes care of the how.

> ***When our energy is caught in resistance to change, we will not change.***

As a woman in her sixth decade of life, I can tell you firsthand that the aging process for women is one that has created a lot of resistance energy. Many women whom I talk to who are approaching mid-life have expressed a lot of fear about getting older. Discussion about how to prevent or delay the process often has these women seeking professional advice on how to stay youthful. The cosmetic industry, anti-aging movement and plastic surgery clinics have created billion-dollar industries that prove my point. I would offer that accepting the real you and loving yourself is the greatest anti-aging treatment on the market.

When our energy is caught in resistance to change, we will not change. It is energy. Remember what you learned: human energy, a.k.a. life force energy, is made up of what you believe, think, say, do, feel and sense. If you resist your present circumstances—whether consciously or unconsciously—you are creating a backlog in your energy, which will hold you hostage until you move into acceptance and allow the energy to move. This is not about self-improvement; this is about self-awareness and shifting mindset to believe you have the power in you to change. Nothing outside of you can change you unless you are willing, consciously or unconsciously, to move toward what you want.

Let me use another example that many of us can relate to. Most of us have lost something or someone in our life. It could be a job, relationship, pet or loved one in death. The ability to move through the emotional energies of that loss is made easier through the energy of acceptance. We cannot change what has happened, as much as we may try. "It is what it is." This may sound cold to anyone who has lost a loved one, but the reality is that the longer you resist the process of grieving, the longer it will take your heart and life to heal. This is where many people will become stuck and blocked in their life as they resist the release of the emotions that are bottled up inside.

Acceptance of your current situation is the catalyst for change. If you cannot accept what you cannot change, you are stuck. If you are stuck and can't find your way out, remember you do not have to do this alone. Seek advice, counsel and healing through whatever means speak to you. This healing process takes a community effort of many stakeholders.

CO-CREATION

We are responsible for creating our life experiences on the level of energy. We are connected to a collective consciousness that will support whatever we focus our attention on, either consciously or unconsciously. However, it must be made clear that we are NOT to blame for our life situation when we don't understand the rules that guide how energy is transformed into experience. During the process of their healing, many of my clients would get angry with me once they became aware of the laws of energy. They said, "So you are telling me this situation is my fault, that I created it." My answer is always "no, it is not your fault. If you don't know better, you can't do better" (remember

> ***We are responsible for creating our life experiences on the level of energy.***

Dr. Phil). However, once you know better and you are aligned with the principles you have learned, you ARE responsible.

In the example with my client and her small living conditions, she was in resistance, even though it was done unconsciously. The collective energy surrounding her picked up on her energy of resistance and want and helped to create her experience, that is, living in her less-than-ideal home. This is exactly how the subconscious mind works. It takes literally our energy (beliefs, thoughts, words, feelings and actions) and transforms it into an experience.

Conversely, when my client shifted into acceptance of her current living situation and felt joy, connection and love for her small space, her next home materialized. Her vision became real because the collective received her direction to create a new field of energy that matched the one she was projecting, hence the manifestation of her heart's desire. This is co-creation. We are working with the energy field that is connected and interconnected to all the energy that exists on the planet. We are not alone.

Trust that the "universe/collective consciousness" is constantly conspiring for your highest and greatest good. It is up to each one of us to send out the right messages so that we receive what we want and need versus what we don't. The universe is listening all of the time, and it gives you exactly what you ask for through the energy you transmit through your life force energy. "Want" creates "want" and "have" creates "have," so pay attention and make sure your signals don't get crossed. Walsch wrote, "That which you want most you push it away by the shear act of wanting it." The energy of having is what will attract it to you. Love and gratitude for the gift of life is a great way to start the energy of "have" to appear.

Trust that the "universe/collective consciousness" is constantly conspiring for your highest and greatest good.

In her book *The Law of Divine Compensation*, Marianne Williamson describes this process beautifully. I highly recommend you read it, along with any other book by Marianne Williamson. She is a powerful thought leader in the area of consciousness and spirituality. In her book *Return to Love*, she has this beautiful and famous quote:

> ***"Our deepest fear is not that we are inadequate. Our deepest fear is that we are powerful beyond measure. It is our Light, not our darkness, that most frightens us."***
> ~ Marianne Williamson

This quote emphasizes the importance of the shadow and light energies I discussed earlier. The fear of our dark side is what prevents us from taking off our mask or persona. The fear of failure, rejection and judgment will keep us wearing a mask until we are fully in touch with our true nature. Once self-love is actualized in our life force, the darkness becomes our opportunity to heal and shift our energy to align with the truth that we are love.

It is extremely important that you take a moment and contemplate what you have just read. Remember, if it does not resonate or make sense to you, then it is not your truth at this time.

However, if you feel that you might be on to something, keep reading to see how to work with this energy of co-creation in a way that has you living your best life. An essential ingredient at this point of your understanding of human energy systems requires you to have a sense of humour. The truth is when life becomes challenging and you pause to reflect on your role in creating the challenge, if you don't learn to laugh you will cry.

Connecting with your true self is a process that does take you on a journey back in time. Uncovering the beliefs that have held you hostage to a life that wasn't being lived to its fullest can literally take you to your knees. Feeling like a victim is a human malady we all experience. You need courage and strength to look at your victim and to embrace and accept that you took on the role as it was taught to you. This is accepting responsibility, which allows you to forgive those that taught it to you. You are able to break the cycle within your family and area of influence by becoming empowered through a healing process that you can be proud of.

Learning to laugh at the voice in your head is required once you are aligned with your conscious mind, your heart and your inner knowing. When you reflect on your past, it is best to do it from a place of discernment. Understand that what happened to you in the past did happen: "it is what it is." However, it is no longer relevant in the present as you move forward in your life. Letting go of what is holding you back is necessary. Getting stuck in shame or blame is not the answer. It is acknowledging, accepting and allowing the memories from the past to move through you to free you from the power they have held over your life.

> ***Understand that what happened to you in the past did happen: "it is what it is." However, it is no longer relevant in the present as you move forward in your life.***

The energy of "forgiveness" is always about acknowledging what has happened and giving yourself permission to process it without having to relive the events. It doesn't mean forgiving the act; it means freeing yourself from the energy that keeps you stuck. For every act of forgiveness, you are empowering yourself to be present and putting you in charge of the moment you are living.

Let me give you a personal example. Through my healing process, I discovered some of my core beliefs growing up included: I didn't matter, and my job was to take care of others, to be a good girl and to be invisible. It worked very well for me until it didn't. In other words, I found myself stuck in my life and it took a healing crisis to wake me up.

Learning about these beliefs had we stunned, as they were unconscious. To anyone who knew me by outer appearances, my life looked perfect. I had a successful career, a wonderful family and good health. If you remember earlier in the book, this was when I discovered I lost my "happy."

I started to seek help and began to do my own inner work. Fast forward to 15 years later, and I am out riding my bike on a trail. I was with my husband who had recently recovered from his illness. We were peddling along, chatting, and my husband took off ahead of me at a quick pace. I could see ahead, and there was on opening in the trail where we had to cross a road that was obstructed by a curve. From where I was on the trail, I could see a car barrelling down the road that my husband couldn't see yet. I started to yell and took my eyes off the trail as I focused on the car through the gap in the trees. Before I knew it, I had hit a gate that was meant to alert riders that a crossing was ahead. My bike made a dead stop and I was thrown over the handlebars headfirst.

As I was lying on the ground, afraid to move, my husband heard me and with a few "interesting" word choices, he rode back to help me. This is what went through my head as I start laughing. "Okay, Universe, I get your message. You need me to stop focusing on others as I have my own path to follow (literally it happened on a path). You are stopping me in my tracks because I am out of alignment again, and you need me to take time to reflect on where I am out of balance." It literally took me less than a minute to get the message. This was no accident. Like I said earlier, the universe is constantly conspiring for my highest and greatest good, even if it has to find a painful way to get my attention.

It took me two weeks to recover from my injuries. I had no broken bones, but both of my wrists were sprained, and I couldn't use them for much more than eating. My husband had to help me dress for a few days. Never once did I feel like a victim. I knew immediately that this was not a coincident or accident; it was perfectly timed for me to notice how my energy was moving out of me rather than in me. The universe also made sure I had enough time to do my own self-care as my energy tank had been depleted through my husband's healing process as I reverted back to being caregiver not self-care receiver.

I have learned that life challenges show up to teach me about healing and understanding the importance of being conscious and present in my daily life. It is hard to break old habits and patterns, so once you begin the journey of healing, it is a life-long commitment to self. Although life challenges can be difficult, the moment you begin to realize the challenge is an opportunity to self-reflect and gain control of your experience, you will begin to see the "silver lining" and do the work.

When life throws you a curve ball, rather than asking "why me," ask "what is this about? What part of me is out of alignment? What part of me am I not loving?" These types of questions always take you deeper into understanding the parts of you that need to be healed and released through consciousness, care and love.

The question "why" should alert you to the habit or pattern of your victim showing up. Why something happens often has only one answer, because it did. In order to figure out "why" something happened, you have to go deeper. Questions that you can ask are: what is this about, whom do I need to talk to, where do I need to go, what can I do to solve this or fix this? You empower yourself to be present and to move through the challenge. The question "why" may lead to an investigation but only when you move to the next question. If you only ask why, your beliefs, thoughts, feelings, words and actions may move to blame, poor me, or speculation that is only based on perception and not truth. The deeper work begins when you move past the "why."

Let me share another personal story with you to illustrate this point. After being with my husband in the hospital for several days, I had to return home to take care of some personal matters. When I arrived in the parking lot, I was shocked to see my car covered in over a foot of snow as there had been a major snowstorm during the critical part of my husband's care when I was unable to leave the hospital. As I stood in front of my car, I thought to myself, "You have to be kidding me—why me?" I soon was overcome with emotion as the tears began to flow. I couldn't get to my snow brush in the car trunk, so I started to frantically clean the snow off my car with my arms and hands.

Part of me felt like a victim of circumstance; however, as I let these feelings flow through me, I suddenly felt a shift in my thoughts and in my heart. I remember thinking that I was glad it was me going through this challenge and not someone else. It was so painful and hard, but I knew I was going to be okay. I remember thinking I would never wish this on another person, and I prayed that I would continue to have the courage to keep on going. It seemed like the minute this feeling moved through me, I noticed movement to my left. A woman was standing beside me, and without saying a word, she was helping me with her snow brush as I cried and released the emotions flowing through me.

When we had finished clearing the snow off the car, she said, "It looks like you have been here for a while. I hope you are okay and whoever you have been here to support is too." I looked at her gratefully and nodded. I thanked her for her kindness and told her that life was hard sometimes but there was always a silver lining if you looked for it.

I realized in that moment that I had shifted my mindset and I felt my heart open to feel the power of being present and accepting the challenge for what it was. It happened—I couldn't change it. However,

I could move through it with grace and dignity, knowing that I was surrounded, protected, guided and directed by a universe that was conspiring for my highest and greatest good.

The lady that helped me was like an angel sent from heaven. Her presence grounded me and helped me to process my situation without judgment. I was able to joke with her and say, "You'd think God gave me enough to deal with, without having to dump a pile of snow on me." We both laughed out loud and then hugged each other. The fresh air, the exercise, the angelic woman and the ability to laugh out loud was just what I needed. When I returned to the hospital later that day, I was a different person and was in the right mindset to support my husband's healing process.

SHADOW WORK

Sharing my client and personal stories with you is to help you understand that challenges will show up in your "emotional energies" and the question "why" won't get you the answers you need. When I saw the snow piled on my car and I asked the question "why me," the immediate thought that came back to me was "why NOT me?"

Challenges happen in all of our lives and when they do, the why isn't relevant, because whatever happened, happened. The answer to why it happened will only be a guess or speculation. For example, when I asked myself "why am I not happy?" the answer that came back was "because you are choosing it." Then I asked "why am I choosing it?" and the answer was still "because you are choosing it."

I had to ask the question differently from my conscious self. I knew I wanted to be happy, so the question then changed to "what would make me happy?" Other questions followed, such as: what does my happy look like and feel like? What would I be doing if I were happy? Who would I be with and what would they be saying about me? Once I answered these questions, I had all kinds of information to use to bring my happy back to me. I empowered myself to become "happy." It now became a state of being rather than a feeling to seek outside myself.

Shadow work is precisely this process—becoming consciously aware of whatever "energy" you are activating through your beliefs, thoughts, words, feelings and actions. The key is "consciousness," as you have now learned from the content of this book. Your subconscious mind works behind the scenes, so if you are not paying attention, you are under the power of this part of your mind. Another name for this might be the "ego mind"/mask/persona. When you are conscious, "self" is in power.

Refer back to the Scale of Emotions chart (in Condition 6), where I identified either fear (shadow) or love (light) emotions. Shadow work is working with the fear-based energies that may be sabotaging your ability to live your best life. For example, if you find yourself in the energy of frustration more times than you would like to be, you will understand that you feel frustrated because you are choosing it as a response to whatever has shown up to challenge you in life. If you want to figure out "why" frustration, you have to ask "what is this about?"

Shadow work is precisely this process—becoming consciously aware of whatever "energy" you are activating through your beliefs, thoughts, words, feelings and actions.

Let me use an example. What happens when you get cut off in traffic? Everyone who drives has had this happen to them, and I know through experience that most people's reaction, including mine, is to become frustrated and angry with the driver who does it to you. The "normal" reaction is to curse and wave a finger at the person, and once you get to your destination to tell everyone about the "idiot" who cut you off and how it made you feel. However, if you paused before you started to get frustrated, you could stop the pattern by simple breathing into your heart and picking a different response. Instead of anger, maybe choose being neutral in your reaction. However you judge another person's behaviour, such as good or bad, is always about them and not you. Your choice to make it personal is a reaction, and your reaction is always about you.

When we take things personally, we are assuming that the person behaving a certain way is intending to do "something" to us. The reality is that your subconscious mind is putting this thought in your head, and you might hear a voice that says something like "who does that person think they are, cutting me off in traffic? Do they think they are more important than I am or they have more important things to do than me?" If this sounds familiar, then you know you have just witnessed "the roommate in your head" (Singer, 2007) taking control.

The truth of the situation is the person who cut you off has no idea who you are, let alone have any opinion about you. They are too busy trying to get where they want to go. They stopped thinking about you once you were in their rearview mirror. You, however, are still carrying around the emotional charge that is affecting you and your day.

The underlying frustration is more about what you think about yourself than the driver of that vehicle. The part of you that feels a victim, or not good enough, was triggered through the emotion of anger and frustration. Thus, if you notice this, you can change it. Simply breathe, pause and let the frustration move through you as you acknowledge the feeling and allow it the space to release. Once you breathe a few more times and notice the voice, you can laugh and tell yourself consciously that the driver must have somewhere to be and you wish him a safe drive. Turn up your tunes and stay neutral, calm and relaxed as you continue to drive.

This is a simple example to give you a chance to work on your emotional energies that make you feel out of balance. Fear-based emotions always have a story or trigger behind them. Something in your past, whether childhood or family dynamics, has created a memory that stored itself in your subconscious and became a habit and pattern for future behaviour.

Fear-based emotions always have a story or trigger behind them.

The previous example is one that repeats itself consistently as we watch our role models behave this way and then we take on the pattern. However, once you notice the pattern, you realize that a car cutting you off simply happened—it is what it is and it has nothing to do with you. Noticing is about you being conscious and self-aware. The next step is moving into the energy of acceptance: it happened and I can't change it. If you can't change what happened and you understand that losing energy over it has no pay off for you, you can then choose how you react from a place of power and balance.

If you notice yourself being triggered into "shadow energies," like frustration, take a moment before you respond. Once you know you are okay and can continue on your drive, stay silent, hold the space and allow your emotions to just move through you. If you are with someone who reacts, stay silent and let their energy move and do not contribute or enable them by adding more energy to support their emotion.

Similar ideas are in a book that I highly recommend, *The Four Agreements* by Don Miguel Ruiz. His subsequent book, *The Fifth Agreement*, is a great addition to the wisdom he shares. The first four agreements are as follows: don't take things personally, don't assume anything, be impeccable with your word and always do your best. The fifth agreement is be skeptical, in other words don't believe everything that you hear. These books are beautifully written, with ease, simplicity and wisdom that will change your life. These books are perfect companions to have if you are on a path to living your best life, as they have instructions on how to work with shadow energies.

It is important to notice that shadow emotions do not feel good. The energy in shadow emotions is often toxic and will mess with your heart, mind and spirit if these emotions are left unchecked. Doing the work required to uncover what is contributing to your emotional responses to life challenges is the key to healing. Again, this goes back to conscious awareness (how do you feel), self-care (what am I going to do about how I feel) and self-love (I am going to do what is necessary because I am worth it). This is when you reach out for support and guidance if you do not feel equipped to handle what is happening in your life.

> ***The energy in shadow emotions is often toxic and will mess with your heart, mind and spirit if these emotions are left unchecked.***

I do not need to remind you about the physical challenges that can arise when we hold onto energies that keep our sympathetic nervous system activated and on high alert. As I mentioned earlier, whenever we are triggered by fear-based emotions, our body's response is to go into "fight or flight" mode. When this happens, our parasympathetic nervous system can no longer manage a homeostatic environment to create harmony and balance in our energy systems. The ability to stay healthy is now compromised if we sustain the "stressed" condition of our fears.

The process of shadow work is critically important as it will identify the stressors in your life and give you an opportunity to manage them through consciousness and care. The shadow process is simple by its very nature, but it is not an easy process because, once again, it requires daily commitment, practice and your conscious intention and attention to reveal and heal the patterns and habits of behaviour that are stressing you out. To get you started, I suggest that you start with emotional energies that are frequently triggered in your life. For example, if you are triggered into anger easily, begin with this emotional energy.

Steps in the shadow process:

1. Conscious awareness: notice emotional energy and label it. For example, I am angry.
2. Create a pause: take a breath.
3. Do not react: keep breathing until you feel yourself calming down and your mind begins to clear. Remember, your reaction or projection is always about you; it is never about the person or situation you are projecting or blaming, even though in your current emotional state (angry) you believe it is their fault.
4. Notice the mind chatter: what is your mind saying to you? What are the thoughts in your busy mind? These thoughts will be clues as to what is underneath the emotion. Here are some examples: it doesn't matter how hard I try, nothing ever works for me! People are so stupid, so why do I even bother to try! Every time I think it will happen for me, things fall through. People are always out to get me. I think you get the idea. You are angry for some reason. When you notice the mind chatter, ask "what is this anger about? Is there a part of me that I am angry at? What am I holding onto that is keeping me angry? Am I really angry at this person/situation or is this about me?"
5. Keep breathing: as you keep breathing and are calming down, notice your energy. Is it shifting? Are you still angry or can you begin to activate a feeling of gratitude and appreciation to open

up your heart so you can feel better about what is happening instead of feeling angry?

6. Journal/write/contemplate/meditate: once your energy has shifted, you are in a place to begin to uncover what is behind the anger. You become a detective for your own healing by asking yourself the questions that focus your attention and intention on releasing the anger so you can feel better and more balanced in your life.

Please note that when you begin using this shadow process, you may have already reacted to the situation. However, in retrospect, you can start the process at Step 6, when you are alone and able to assess the situation and how you reacted. It is important to notice the habit and pattern of behaviour or feeling that you want to change. Your conscious awareness is the key, and the process is secondary. The more you practise, the more you will be able to diffuse the emotional energy.

Over time, your reaction will gradually dissipate until eventually you don't react at all. This is when you know you have a tool that can keep your energy in balance and harmony whenever you need it. It is always one breath at a time. Remember that this work is about you and for you. Your health and balance must be first and foremost in your mind. Staying balanced through attention to your "self" will ensure the foundational health of your physical body. This is a motivator to do the work.

Understanding the "shadow" process empowers you. Through practice, you can take back control when you are triggered by emotions that take you out of your heart and into your head. When life begins to challenge you, instead of reacting you now have a process you can follow consciously to take you out of a difficult situation into a less difficult one.

Releasing old emotional energies frees up your energy systems within your physical body to be replaced with more neutral and calming frequencies. These emotional releases support the foundational pillar of your physical structures, and health and wellness improve substantially. Also remember that your parasympathetic nervous system brings balance and harmony to the physical body so healing can occur. The breath, connection to the heart and calming the busy monkey mind take you out of "stress" a.k.a. sympathetic nervous system to parasympathetic, where your body regulates and balances.

Anger is one of those emotions that can be a double-edged sword. Anger moves energy, which is good when it is expressed in appropriate ways. However, anger turned inward—that is repressed and suppressed—will at some point in time be expressed inappropriately both in timing and magnitude. I am sure many of you have been on the receiving end of someone losing their mind inappropriately when you simply said the wrong word or triggered a deeply buried emotion.

Recognize that someone else's "bad" behaviour is always about them and how you respond to their bad behaviour is always about you. Learning to pause and not react will go a long way to avert conflict. Heart energy will activate compassion. This will allow you to stay balanced while holding space for the person who has lost their mind to the anger. This is an important tool to use for conflict resolution when in relationship with others. It is also how you heal yourself.

Recognize that someone else's "bad" behaviour is always about them and how you respond to their bad behaviour is always about you.

If emotions that are suppressed and repressed nest in the physical body, then shouldn't everyone be instructed on how to move these energies in order to create balance and harmony? We know energy is creative, so if energy is not moving, what happens to these stagnant emotional energies that we hold onto? Remember my client who had the pain in his neck? Can you imagine how different his life would have been had he released the energy of his father's judgment before he ended up needing surgery to heal it?

Through 5,000 years of study and practice, Eastern medicine has identified various areas of the body where emotions will disrupt, block, congest, constrict, or stagnate the flow of energy. This understanding suggests that the symptoms of illness and disease can have energetic connections. For example, the emotions that nest in the area of the heart would be feelings of abandonment, betrayal, heartache, love unreceived, effort unreceived and vulnerability, to name a few. Emotions that can nest in the detox organs like the liver, bladder and kidneys would be anger, frustration, conflict, bitterness, resentment, taken for granted, hatred, depression, guilt, unsupported and fear, just to name a few.

If there is even the slightest possibility that emotional energies stored in the body can contribute or cause some physical "dis-ease," then shouldn't we be spending time learning how to release these old energies, while at the same time learning to release them as they happen?

This is a two-fold process. If we don't acknowledge and release what we are holding onto, it will only create more of what it is. Until we learn to acknowledge the old pattern or habits of belief and thought and delete them from the subconscious programs that exist, we will stay stuck. Another book I recommend that you read is *When the Body Says No* by Dr. Gabor Mate. This book shares stories of how certain "personality" types have manifested certain "dis-eases" and how some people were able to improve their health by changing behaviour and belief.

Bringing shadow emotions into the light allows the subconscious mind to do a memory sweep of the emotional energies that are no longer serving our health and balance.

The understanding that our body will be impacted by our emotional traumas and beliefs emphasizes the importance of self-awareness, care and love. This is something we can all manage and control if we pay attention and do our own work to strength the pillars that hold up the foundation for our health and wellness.

Bringing shadow emotions into the light allows the subconscious mind to do a memory sweep of the emotional energies that are no longer serving our health and balance. Once these emotions are released, the new subconscious programs can be designed around staying neutral or moving our energy into our hearts, where the energy is expansive and healing. As these heart energies move through our body systems, unimpeded old beliefs and thoughts are replaced with new improved ones that encourage and inspire us to live our best life.

This shadow process is a tool to be used daily. I wish I could tell you that this is easy to do. It is not. Staying present and doing your work every day to stay in the energy of your heart and out of your busy monkey mind is a lifetime commitment once you start down this path. I work in energy every day, and every day I am challenged in my own life to practise the work I teach.

Staying present and aware of what you feel is key to the process. I constantly say "what you feel is real"; all the rest of the stuff is just mind clutter. When you don't feel good, you have to move your energy towards what does feel good to feel better. The decision is always yours. The timing and the tools you use to move your energy are within you and can only be powered by you.

> ***The shadow process teaches you that life challenges are opportunities for healing.***

It doesn't matter how many books you read, courses you take, webinars you listen to or coaches you work with, the healing process only begins when you do your work. Work is not a four-letter word that needs to be dreaded. Work is energy. It is the movement towards something. If you are in a holding pattern and waiting for something to happen, that is where you will stay. However, if you move toward something by making a decision and then working that decision, you will find that life will begin to open up for you in ways you would never have imagined possible.

Asking for help, seeking answers and then doing your work is all part of the process. This is not a job to be done alone, but it is an inside-out type of process. Turning your eyes inward and digging through the story of your life, not to relive it but to revive it, will set you on a path to healing so you can live your best life.

The shadow process teaches you that life challenges are opportunities for healing. The easy stuff, the good stuff in life, is awesome and also a reminder that this is how you want to live your life. However, the challenges and the mistakes that are made along the path are what create the opportunity to change your mind, to shift perspective, to follow a different path and eventually to find your way home. Being upset and angry allows you to find peace and tranquility when you do the work to find the seed of your upset and your anger. To live life in the shadows is a waste when there is so much to do in the light.

SUMMARY

You are it. Everything that you need or want in your life is already in you. The way to access this knowing and this truth is to:

1. Take a breath.
2. Create a pause and slow down your "monkey mind."
3. Keep breathing until your busy mind calms and clears.
4. Drop into the energy of your heart by activating "feelings" of gratitude and appreciation.
5. Focus on the breath and the feeling you are generating in the power plant of your being—your heart.
6. Feel the expansion in your heart energy and know that that feeling is the "real" you. The energy of wonder and beauty that you came into the world with is your true nature. It is love and it is YOU.
7. From this place of conscious knowing, become the person you were meant to be. Breathe into any of life challenges, knowing that you can move through whatever it is because your power comes from your heart.
8. The power plant of your experience is the energy that your heart can generate when you are connected to the good that is in your life and the good that surrounds you in the collective consciousness of those who are like-minded.
9. Hold space for yourself and know that you are the one who gets to decide in each moment who, what and how you will move through this moment.
10. The blueprint of your gifts, passion and purpose resides in your heart. When you connect with your conscious breath, you have the ability to activate your heart energy so you can tap into your genius and then live your best life.
11. Believe this as truth and know that the power to change your life begins now.

Chapter Four

STRATEGIES TO LIVE YOUR BEST LIFE

This part of the book will outline some strategies, exercises and suggestions to guide you on the path to living your best life. Each strategy has been developed through connecting with the data, information and knowledge that have been outlined in the previous pages of this book. You might want to call these strategies "tools" that you can use when you find yourself losing focus and need to readjust your "energy" to find the balance and harmony that are missing to keep you on track.

You might want to call these strategies "tools" that you can use when you find yourself losing focus and need to readjust your "energy" to find the balance and harmony that are missing to keep you on track.

Understanding the mechanism of your mind and how it functions in consciousness and subconsciousness is a key to unlocking the gateway to your heart and the power it controls to fuel your life. The information about the human energy system offers you an opportunity to take full control of your "physical vehicle" by practising conscious awareness of "self." Using your intention to connect with the emotional energies that promote healing will provide opportunities to shift your perspective/ mindset in order to develop new habits and patterns of behaviour that will support you living your best life.

Focusing on the foundational requirements for health and wellness is a personal commitment that can be brought into balance only through the conscious effort to know your "self." Being self-ish is an important part of healing the past and knowing that you are the answer to everything you are seeking, wanting, needing and achieving in your life.

I would remind you that the process of healing, although personal, should not be done alone or in isolation. The resources that are available to you require you to make the decision to reach out and seek the support and guidance that will get you to your goal when you find yourself stuck or stalled in your progress. There are health-care professionals, nutritionists/dietitians, personal trainers, alternative health care practitioners/coaches, spiritual and religious counsellors and other support people who are ready and available when you decide assistance is needed. There is also a wealth of information in books, webinars and on-line forums that are easy to research and find through intention and effort.

Learning to live your best life is about moving your "energy" forward through intention, effort and work. The following "tools" are meant to guide you to create a vision for your best life, so you begin living it now.

THE CONSCIOUS BREATH

The first strategy is learning how to connect with the part of you that holds the blueprints for your passion and purpose in life. The heart is the energy centre that holds this information, and the breath is the mechanism that will bring your attention and intention to reveal its secrets.

The separation of our "self" from our heart energy is a major contributor to feeling disconnected from our passion and purpose. This was demonstrated repeatedly with the hundreds of clients that I have worked with as well as with my own healing process. Working with the Emotion Code and heart wall protocols, I was able to witness a positive shift in my clients' emotional energies when their heart wall was removed. Once the emotional traumas and memories of the past were released from the area of their heart, the energy boost opened up the higher frequency feelings that motivated and moved them towards discovering the gifts and talents that they possessed and had forgotten.

I highly recommend the website *discoverhealing.com*. There is a Practitioner Map that you can scroll through and find someone you might want to work with. Working with a trained practitioner is a good investment when you are struggling to heal the past. The Emotion and Body Code are amazing tools for transformation and healing.

I remember reading in Neale Donald Walsch's *Conversation with God* a section on "knowing self." He said that "what is of God is in me." This translated for me to mean that everything I needed was already in me. However, based on what I had learned about energy, I had disconnected from "knowing self" when I separated from my heart and my connection to this Higher Power. I began to wonder what parts of me I had forgotten. When I read that section in the book, it was one of those "take a breath" moments for me. It spoke directly to my heart and I asked the question, "What have I forgotten?"

The separation of our "self" from our heart energy is a major contributor to feeling disconnected from our passion and purpose.

This was a time when I actually took the question above into a meditation. I call this practice a "breathing exercise" for those who are uncomfortable with the thought of doing a meditation. I sat quietly, closed my eyes and kept breathing and relaxing and repeating the question. As I sat with my breath, in and out, and the question, my mind cleared, and I started to feel things I had forgotten. My heart started to expand, and I experienced that feeling of "bliss" I shared earlier in the book.

As the question "what have I forgotten?" reached my heart through my breath, I started to have flashes of memory that reminded me of my "child-like" wonder about the world. The books I used to read as a child were about mystery, fantasy, discovery, magical beings and the great mystery of life. As the feeling of connection to this grew, I knew it was a clue to my passion and purpose. I felt like my magical thinking as a child and the mystery and intrigue of discovery were part of the gift I carry.

Using your breath to take you into your heart energy is a key strategy to discover your true nature and your "self" at a much deeper level. If you struggle with this breathing and connection, it could mean you have some work to do to release old stagnant memories or traumas of the past that have closed your heart off to the good things in your life.

Using your breath to take you into your heart energy is a key strategy to discover your true nature and your "self" at a much deeper level.

Here are a few suggestions to help with this process, especially the heart-based breathing process that I outlined earlier in the book and I will repeat here:

HEART-BASED BREATHING

The Purpose: The purpose of the breathing is to consciously connect your mind to the present moment. Focusing on the heart drops our busy mind (subconscious chatter) into the expansive energy of the heart (super conscious mind). This then connects us to the physical body with the deep intention to release trapped memories, programs, habits or patterns from the subconscious mind and the physical body. The energy of the heart radiates an electromagnetic signal into the energy field around you. Connection to this energy will allow the release of memories with ease and gentleness as we learn to focus on what we want versus what we don't want.

The Process: Take a breath to calm, slow down and relax and then begin to focus on the area of the heart (place your hand over your heart if it helps you to focus). Imagine breathing into the heart, and then activate a feeling of gratitude or appreciation and begin to feel your energy shift. Pay attention to what the shift in energy feels like for you. Do you feel tingling or a feeling of expansion in your heart; do you feel a warmth, calmness or peacefulness? Whatever you are feeling is unique to you, and you are receiving a clue to what your "spirit/ life force energy" feels like when you are connected to your heart and energy field around you. This is healing energy that will create the opportunity to shift and change habits and patterns of belief, thought, feeling and behaviour that no longer serve you.

THE EMOTION CODE

The Emotion Code is a book written by Dr. Bradley Nelson. I highly recommend you read it as it is a wonderful resource to connect to the process of emotional releases and the heart wall work. I believe everyone should have a copy of this book in their home to support preventative healing options when emotional traumas are holding you hostage in your life. It can be ordered through online retailers or from the website *www.discoverhealing.com*.

MINDFULNESS MEDITATIONS

Definition: Mindfulness meditation is a mental training practice that involves focusing your mind on your experiences (like your own emotions, thoughts and sensations) in the present moment. Mindfulness meditation can involve breathing practice, mental imagery, awareness of body and mind, and muscle and body relaxation (*wikipedia.org*).

This definition encompasses a great deal of information. There are many on-line versions on how to do mindfulness mediation, and I would suggest that you simply research the best method for you.

Guided meditations tapes are available on-line and in bookstores. This process also provides a great way to connect with your heart and get into the practice of using your conscious breath to shift your energy into a calm and peaceful energy where healing will begin.

HEARTMATH INSTITUTE

The HeartMath Institute empowers individuals, families, groups and organizations to enhance their life experiences using tools that enable them to better recognize and access their intuition and heart intelligence.

I highly recommend connecting with the HeartMath Institute to anyone who is interested in the scientific research on the intelligence of the heart. Their website (*heartmath.org*) provides many resources as well as their products, which have been on the market for well over 25 years and have served to educate many of us on the importance of connecting with our heart energy to create a better life and world.

GLOBAL COHERENCE INITIATIVE

The Global Coherence Initiative is an amazing organization that has worked with the HeartMath Institute to inform and educate those who have connected around the qualities of the heart and its healing power not only for the individual but also for our planet. I highly recommend that you connect with *heartmath.org* to gain insight and understanding of the power you possess to improve your health and wellness. This is a message I recently received from the Global Coherence Initiative that I think says it all:

> *"We know our hearts help to heal us, connect us and influence the fundamental good of the world we share. Qualities of the heart such as empathetic care, kindness and compassion are among the most uplifting and empowering energy we can experience. Studies are proving the benefits and effectiveness of these qualities and how to use them to maximize our full human potential to become who we truly are.*
>
> *"During these obvious transitional times, people are increasingly seeking solutions to calm their anxiety, relieve their fears, and reduce their stress. Stress has become a priority issue now."*

DAILY PRACTICES

A simple way for you to begin the process of connecting with your "self" and beginning to take control of your feelings and emotions is to set up daily practices that you repeat and practise consciously until they become automatic.

The practices I am talking about are ones that work on shifting mindset and belief patterns through consciousness. It requires you to set up daily routines in which you set the intention and focus to shift your energy into the heart using your breath and self-awareness to guide the routine. My personal morning practice is not to get out of bed until I am fully awake and conscious and I have set up energetically what my day will be and become.

MORNING PRACTICE

Each morning as my eyes open and I let the world in, I stretch my physical body, much like any animal will do when they awake from a deep sleep. This awakens the body and alerts me to any pain or stiffness that needs a few extra moments to regulate and balance. I always take two or three deep breaths and then I set my intention to start my day with thoughts of appreciation and gratitude for a new day.

I reflect on what I would like to accomplish for the day and the energy to make it happen seamlessly with ease and gentleness. I connect with the right "attitude" or mindset to accomplish the tasks at hand and picture the outcome exactly the way I want them to be. I have a little prayer that I offer to the universe to ask for support and guidance in living my day to the fullest. Only when I am satisfied that I have set the stage energetically for a day that is inspired and that I will aspire to do my best, then and only then do I get up and out of bed.

This practice initially took me several minutes, but after many days, months and years of doing this, it now takes only a few seconds to get me motivated and ready to go. I find myself waking up with a smile on my face and grateful for the day ahead. Even when my body, mind and spirit may be running a bit low, I can find something to focus my attention and intention on to move me into a better feeling that will support me throughout the day.

EVENING PRACTICE

A similar routine can be repeated before sleep as well. Make sure you set yourself up for a wonderful sleep by calming and relaxing the mind before bed. Separate yourself from technology and other busy work a few hours before bedtime. Have a calming drink like tea, water or warm milk before bed to help relax the mind and body.

Once you are in bed, take a few moments to cycle through your day and focus on the high points of the day and things or people you are grateful for. Do not let your mind take you to the challenges and the "woulda, coulda, shoulda" thoughts that will cycle through your mind and keep you awake at night. Breathe deeply and fully and notice where you feel tension in your physical body. Stretch your body and then relax it, setting the intention to release any energy that is not serving you. Breathe and relax, breathe and relax and then release your body and mind to the night and the sleep that awaits you.

ONE-MINUTE REBOOT

While working or engaged in busy work, give yourself 60 seconds every hour to stop what you are doing. This practice helps to create a pause in your schedule to stretch, move and breathe. This one-minute reboot creates a pause in whatever you are doing so that you can assess how you are feeling.

Often, we will work endlessly until we finish a job or a project, sometimes to the point of exhaustion. Many people will just put their head down and plow through a task, often resulting in mistakes and missteps that can lead to frustration and anger. The one-minute reboot signals that you are doing some self-care to move energy and to notice how your physical body feels and if your mind is still connected to your power centre. The reboot creates the pause so you can make decisions either to continue your work or not, so that you can get back on track to accomplish what you want and need. Giving yourself permission to take these little breaks can be hugely supportive and beneficial for sustaining and maintaining your energy through long hours of works, whether at home or at your place of business.

JOURNALING

Writing has always been cathartic for me. It allows me to express myself in the moment and then to have a resource to return to in the future when I need to re-remember where I started from. It is much like writing a letter to a friend or family member. I began journaling over 20 years ago to track my healing journey and progress through the years. My journals have become a resource and a source of comfort to me when I reflect on my life. Journaling is now a natural part of my daily routine.

I suggest you get yourself a journal or notebook so that you can begin to document the important things you discover about yourself.

As you write down what you think, feel and do on a daily basis, you create a record of where you are at and also where you might like to go. You can have different journals for different areas of your life, for example, a dream journal or a gratitude journal. I would offer that you create a "Me Journal" and make it all about you as you begin to figure out how to live your best life.

PAY ATTENTION

Pay attention is referring to your "consciousness" and staying in the present, rather than letting your monkey mind run amok with thoughts that have you stuck in the past or in an emotional energy that is not good for you. Pay attention means you are focusing on the day-to-day occurrences while you move towards whatever goals you have set for yourself.

This is where your journal can be fun to use, as you begin to write down interesting occurrences throughout the course of your day. For example, write down whenever you notice a change in your behaviour. Many of my clients shared anecdotes with me about how something had happened during the day and they didn't overreact to it, whereas in the past they would lose their minds.

Also notice things in your outer world to see if the universe might be sending you a message. For example, a particular song comes on the radio and it reminds you of a person you have been meaning to get in touch with and you pick up the phone and call them. Once you connect, the person tells you they were just thinking of you too. Or an animal or bird crosses your path and you decide to look up the "spiritual meaning" of this particular "chance meeting" and discover the meaning has a message that you needed to hear in that moment. Another example is reading billboards, signs on trucks or books that are recommended, all of which have a message that guides and supports you in the moment.

Documenting these types of occurrences is validating that you are shifting out of your "subconscious" automatic responses to life and you are living more fully in the present, which allows you to take charge of your experiences from a place of self-awareness, care and love.

SHADOW WORK

Shadow work begins when we become consciously aware of how we react to the life challenges that show up in our daily life. Whenever we are triggered by a person, situation or experience and begin to react by projecting or blaming in the lower frequency emotional energies, it is the cue to "take a breath" and begin the shadow process. The lower frequency emotional energies are the ones steeped in feelings of fear and are remnants of memories and traumas from the past. The shadow emotions never feel good. That is a clue for you to take that first breath to create a pause, so that you can drop into the feeling you are experiencing and question whether it is something you want to feel or not. The energy shift only comes when you consciously ask yourself if the reaction is appropriate to the present situation and what and who do you want to be in the moment.

> ***Whenever we are triggered by a person, situation or experience and begin to react by projecting or blaming in the lower frequency emotional energies, it is the cue to "take a breath" and begin the shadow process.***

The breath creates the pause and pulls you into the present, so you are watching yourself react versus reacting. It gives you the opportunity to decide from a different viewpoint or perspective to be the person you want to be versus repeating a habit or pattern of behaviour that does not serve you well.

The shadow practices are the most transformational in the process of connecting you with yourself and understanding the parts of you that need to be healed. The shadow work is the part of the healing process that focuses on discovering and releasing the emotional memories and traumas from the past that are preventing you from living your best life now.

The steps to use in your daily shadow practice are:

1. Connect to your consciousness (notice how you feel).
2. Breathe.
3. Pause.
4. Identify the shadow emotion/fear-based emotion. Refer to the Scale of Emotions chart with the list of shadow emotions for

guidance. Give yourself permission to feel the emotion and allow it to move through your energy field.

5. Activate heart-based breathing.
6. Shift your consciousness to appreciation and gratitude.
7. Decide to release the shadow emotion(s) and replace with a "lighter emotion." You want to move into a feeling that is gentler and will ease you into a calmer and more balanced state.
8. Repeat this process for every "trigger" that you can manage on a daily basis.
9. Journal these experiences.

When you practise this shadow work process, you will see over time that each time you practise, the challenges will become less and less until you no longer react the same way to that particular person, situation or experience. You are learning and teaching yourself to stay in the energy of your heart, where you are in control and have the power to stay balanced and feel good about your life. You will also notice that this process will become automatic or subconscious, as you have set up a new program that is instructing your subconscious mind to stay in the lighter emotional energies or in your heart. You will begin to notice that you react less and less to your outside world as your inner world begins to regulate and calibrate to the energy of your heart and what you want in your life.

Life challenges and shadows are the opportunities for you to practise being in the energy of your heart and finding a different way of being.

Remember that physical health challenges can be a message that you are out of balance. Your sympathetic nervous system is activated and your parasympathetic is shut down, leading to "energy" depletion or overload. This is the "shadow" showing up and inviting you to use your consciousness to make decisions to use the tools available to you so you can change your condition. Always begin with the "breath" and allow it to guide you to a plan to find balance.

Life challenges and shadows are the opportunities for you to practise being in the energy of your heart and finding a different way of being. The areas of your life where you have placed limitations or judgments are the jewels to the healing process and give you the knowledge and ability to release the old patterns of thought and behaviour and create new ones. This is when you open your life up to new possibilities and begin to live your best life.

VISION, MISSION AND VALUES

The exercise to develop a vision, mission and values statement requires time and effort to dig deep into the qualities and traits you possess that matter and move you in your life. One of the hardest things for me to do on this path was to turn my eyes inward to rediscover what I had forgotten about myself. For others, this may not be a difficult task. Nonetheless, it is an important and necessary exercise to get in touch with your "self."

Learning to know the person you are by focusing on the things that you want in your life starts by doing an honest self-analysis, using exercises like the one from Stephen Covey, which I outlined earlier in the book. I would highly recommend that you do this exercise to get you practising the heart-based breathing and connecting to the energy of your heart. When you are in the energy of your heart, you will feel yourself opening up to the parts of you that make you feel excited and happy about your life.

At the end of the exercise, you will have a list of qualities and traits that you can aspire to be come. This list will also allow you to re-remember that these traits are the truth of who you are and will forever guide you on your path to living your best life.

Another great exercise is to spend time answering the following six questions:

1. What are my strengths?

This question is extremely important in knowing your "self" and knowing what gifts, talents and even passions that you carry in your "soul." Being consciously aware of these strengths provides data, information and knowledge that can guide you in the direction of your purpose and living your best life.

A tool I used that was extraordinarily accurate and instrumental in my current work was the CliftonStrengths at *gallop.com*. This assessment tool identifies your strengths and potential based on the information you provide through a survey process. What I discovered about myself was incredibly useful, and it mirrored the qualities that I do possess, but I was not in tune with them or aware how they were working in my life.

Let me give you an example. The number one theme in my assessment is "connectedness." The description of this strength is: "*People who are especially talented in the Connectedness theme have faith in the links between all things. They believe there are few coincidences and that almost every event has a reason. A person with this trait senses that they are linked to all humanity.*"

When I read this, it blew me away because it so accurately described what I believed about life and all living organisms. It explained my drive to learn, research and prove this belief through the study of energy, consciousness, healing, spirituality and science. My curiosity and desire to understand had me shifting my career and passion in the direction of what I loved and felt passionate about.

The most interesting outcome of understanding my own strengths was to bring me to the realization that they were personal and unique to me. As an energy practitioner, that was a huge "take a breath" moment. In working with clients, I began to understand why some of the concepts and principles I was teaching were sometimes difficult to grasp. My belief and perception of interconnectedness was a truth for me, but it was not necessarily a strength or truth of my clients. Once I understood this, I was able to gear my sessions towards the individual and walk them through my process at the pace and depth that they felt comfortable with. I began to offer a free 30-minute consult so that potential clients could see the way I worked and understood the principles and concepts of healing I was offering. If someone didn't resonate with me energetically through this consult, we both were satisfied that we were not meant to work together.

What I also came to realize was that in my former career as a human resource manager, the recruitment process would have benefited so much more with assessment tools that would identify the strengths of employees. So often through hiring practices, people are recruited into jobs that they are not suited for and end up either unhappy or unproductive in their jobs due to lack of skill, desire and passion. If an employer had a clear picture of an employee's strengths, they could match the person to the right type of job. I remember that so many people who moved through the ranks of a company would end up in positions, especially management, for which they did not have the leadership qualities or people skills to be successful. The amount of time, effort and money spent to try to get the person trained would often fail because it was not a strength that they possessed.

This now has me believing that all the self-improvement information out there might have it backwards. There is no need for self-improvement; there is simply a greater need to know yourself, your strengths and your passions. The best way to do that is open your heart and move towards what you discover about yourself. If you can connect to your gifts, skills, talents, passions, dreams and desires, your ability to live your best life is within reach. However, if you feel you have lost that connection, then I highly recommend doing the CliftonStrengths Assessment at *gallup.com.*

Let's move on to the next question.

2. What are my weaknesses? This is not to identify where you need self-improvement; it is to identify areas that may be blocked or stuck or to show you areas that are not your genius. This information is helpful to know and will support you on the path towards what you want to achieve in your life. Remember, I discovered that my genius wasn't painting, but it helped me identify which of my skills and abilities were stronger.

3. Ask a trusted friend, colleague or family member what they think your strengths and weaknesses are. Hopefully, they will be honest and forthright, but realize that this is only an opinion. It is important you have a sense of what others do think about you to ensure you are representing the person you want to be.

4. Who are some of the people you admire the most in life? Make a list, and beside their name list the traits that you admire and why. Then ask yourself if you too possess that trait.

Remember, through the laws of energy, the truth is "if you spot a trait, you got the trait!" The laws of energy are specific to the letter. If a frequency of energy is something that you see, feel, touch, think and believe, then the frequency will attract what is "like" it back to you. This is the Law of the Circle, also known as the Law of Attraction.

Understand that when you see a trait, behaviour or quality in another, whether you label it good or bad, you also possess it. Refer to the Scale of Emotions earlier in the book to remind you that every emotion exists within your human energy system. In the case of admiring a quality in someone else, it means that you too possess that quality, and if you haven't activated it in you, then now is your chance to empower yourself to do so.

This is exciting stuff. When you write down a name like Oprah Winfrey and you say you admire her because she is generous of heart, intelligent and powerful, guess what? So are you! And if you aren't behaving that way, this is now your chance to activate your power centre and start moving and working towards the goals that will get you where you want to be.

When I say activate your power centre, this means a "take a breath" moment. Drop into the energy of your heart and expand your heart so it begins to open up to the field of energy that surrounds you. The sea of possibilities lies in the space that surrounds you. If you are familiar with Albert Einstein's work, you will know that his greatest discoveries happened when he was in a meditative state, allowing himself to free his mind and open his heart to the collective energy surrounding him. In this space of "freedom," the inspiration of new ideas and possibilities creates the opportunity for mysteries to be solved and new discoveries to be found.

Having said this, there is more detective work that you need to do. Let's continue asking questions and filling in the blanks to discover your purpose, passion and gifts that you might not know that you carry.

5. What are your favourite books to read and TV shows that you watch? Personally, I love fantasy, magical worlds, murder, mystery and intrigue. I love to solve puzzles, mysteries and whodunit thrillers. When I started my research into spirituality and connection to the Divine during my husband's illness, the books I started to read were about hands-on healing, Eastern medicine, energy, mediumship, intuition, consciousness, and native traditions and culture. My world began to expand, and my passion and purpose began to unfold.

6. What are some of your hobbies and pastimes that you enjoy and make you feel more connected and happy in your life? These activities are clues to pay attention to and do more often. Once you feel this connection, it will lead you to your passion, purpose and gifts that you carry and need to share with the world.

If walking in nature is a favourite pastime, then the next time you take a hike through the woods, bring a note pad, journal or voice recorder and spend time connecting to how you feel and record it so that you can recreate that feeling no matter what you are doing. The reverse question is "what are some of the activities that you do not enjoy and why?"

I will give you an example. I never enjoyed cooking while I was in my busy life with career and family. I dreaded having to figure out meal plans, shopping and then preparing the family meals. There was an undercurrent of resentment and anger that it was my responsibility. However, when I discovered the "energy" of my happy, I realized that feeding my family and self was a very important responsibility. For those years when I prepared meals feeling resentment and anger, I now understand—through the laws of energy—that I was putting that energy into the food I prepared. When I made a decision to "accept" my responsibility with my "happy" energy, I began to set the stage to cook and feel the joy of doing so. At first, it wasn't easy, but over time I began to look forward to this time of the day. Once I started to pay more attention and stay present, the meals I prepared actually started to taste better.

When I prepare a meal now, I focus on the task at hand. I am more organized and present. When I am cutting carrots and making a salad, I pay attention and am fully conscious and aware of what I am doing. I think about the food as nourishing my family and sustaining our health and balance. I feel appreciation and gratitude for the farmers and workers who make the food available for me. I now look at food preparation as an opportunity to stay present and be happy. I am grateful that I can afford good food and have a family to share it with. I will admit that the days I am not "feeling it," we go out for dinner, no judgment, just self-care.

Although cooking is not my passion nor my purpose in life, it is something I can do now that is activated from the energy of my heart. I am no longer lost in my "head" thinking about all the reasons why I hated doing it, which was probably poisoning myself and my family in the process.

Once you have answered all these questions to the best of your ability and you feel connected to the information, then you are ready to set up your vision for your life.

VISION EXERCISES

Earlier in my book I talked about creating a field of possibilities. I used the example of a designer and how they will conceive of an idea, then create it through a design process that involves stages of development until it is a reality. The "energy" of intention is the dynamic that will get the process moving.

Creating your vision requires the same type of process. The vision you create for your life begins first in your imagination as an idea, dream or desire. The vision begins where you are now (acceptance) and then develops when you focus your intention and attention on all the things you want in your life. The goal of your vision is to set the stage so that all you dream of will become a reality.

It's much like the designer who has an idea for a chair. He does not focus on what already exists, he focuses on the idea of a "new" chair by creating the parameters of what the chair's purpose and use will be. All the chairs that currently exist are the springboard for the inspiration for the next version, style, design or function of the next chair. Your vision is about the process of developing your own version of what already exists.

Let me share with you a personal story that will bring more clarity to what I am proposing. Early in our marriage, my husband and I relocated to a new town to follow a career opportunity. It was a new adventure, and both of us were excited to begin our married life in a new community. At first, it was difficult leaving our families and friends, but then we settled into our new life, eager to set our own path, establish connection and put down some roots.

My husband started his new job, and within a week or two, his boss invited us to his home to meet his family and enjoy a meal to help us settle in. It was a lovely visit, and we both enjoyed ourselves immensely. After we left, both of us talked about the experience.

We both hoped that our marriage would endure the test of time as this couple's had. They had been married for well over 20 years and had two beautiful daughters and a warm, inviting and cozy home in a community that felt like home. As the years went by, I often thought about that experience and realized that I was creating much of the same energy in my own life. At the time of writing this book, our marriage has endured the test of time, and we have three beautiful daughters who are married with families. We all live in a community that feels like home.

The vision that I had for my life is not the same as the one that my husband's boss had for his. However, he created the field for me to see the possibilities of what could happen in my life if I focused my attention and intention on the things I liked and wanted from his experience. Sometimes you might not know what you want until something or someone comes into your life and inspires you to reach for the stars.

The important message here is that when you focus on what you want, you will often attract it into your life through the laws of energy, as your conscious and subconscious mind has already created the field for it to show up. When we focus on what we don't want, guess what? The conscious and subconscious mind will create the field to match what you don't want. Therefore, your vision must come from the energy of your heart, and then it will manifest over time through effort, focus and passion on your part.

The phrase "act as if" is the "energy" I am referring to above. When you "act as if," you are living your dream, no matter what your circumstances might be. You are "creating the field" for it to grow and develop. An exercise that I found extremely valuable in the process of creating a field for my vision was a process introduced to me when I trained and certified in the Psych-K protocols.

The practice was to complete a VAK to the Future worksheet (*psych-k.com*). This worksheet is designed to help you focus on setting goals that you want into the future. Each "goal" requires you to use Visual, Auditory and Kinesthetic (VAK) cues to visualize the goal now as if it already existed. Let me give you an example.

Let's say that the goal you want is to be in a loving relationship. Currently, you are not, but this is a goal that you want in your life.

The first step in setting up the field for this goal/vision is to ask yourself this question: "What will I SEE in my life that will let me know that I have achieved this goal?" Now list three things. The parameters for this list must be that you SEE it now, so you are not in the picture, you are creating the picture.

For example, the first thing you might SEE (visual cues) is you sitting across from your partner at a restaurant. You can see your hands in front of you, and you are holding hands. Your partner is smiling and laughing as you talk about your day. The second thing you SEE is yourself holding hands with your partner as you stroll through a park. You see your hand enclosed in your partner's and the smile on their face tells you that you are happy and enjoying each other's company. The third thing might be that you SEE yourself in a church, and you are standing in front of all the guests with your partner and a ring is sliding onto your finger as you exchange vows.

The next part of the exercise is to use auditory cues that will tell you that your goal/vision is a reality. You would ask these two questions: "What do I HEAR people saying about me now that I am in a loving relationship? What am I HEARING myself say about me because of this loving relationship? For example, you might HEAR your friends and family say, "Ever since you met (your partner), you are so happy and upbeat. You always have a smile on your face and you are so content and confident in all that you do." Things you might HEAR yourself say to others might be "I look forward to every day now. I am so excited about my life and where I am headed. It is so nice to have someone to share my dreams with and to be with someone who gets me. I am so blessed and content to be me right now."

The third step is to focus on kinesthetic cues (feelings) that relate to you being in a loving relationship now. You would ask yourself, "How do I FEEL? Have I ever FELT this FEELING before in my life?" Let's say the FEELING is "JOY." Close your eyes and remember when you last felt "joy." Once you find the memory and activate the FEELING of JOY in your physical body, fill in the blanks below.

Where do I FEEL joy in my body the most?

If this FEELING is a colour, what colour would it be?

If this FEELING is a shape, what shape would it be?

If this FEELING has a temperature, would it be hot, cold or warm?

If this FEELING has a texture, how does it FEEL when I touch it?

The answers to these questions might be "I FEEL joy in my heart and when I FEEL it, it FEELS expansive like a huge bubble that surrounds my body. When I FEEL joy, I see bursts of colour like fireworks, and the texture is cool and smooth like silk."

Once you have completed this exercise, you are now ready to develop a belief statement that will match the visual, auditory and kinesthetic qualities you have experienced as a result of having a loving relationship. Belief statements are "energy" and will be stored as a subconscious program once the conscious mind accepts it as a truth. Therefore, a belief statement must be stated in the first person and in the present tense; it is true or will be true in the future ("act as if").

Here are some examples of a belief statement that would support your goal to be in a loving relationship: "I am worthy of an intimate, loving relationship," or "I am clear about what I want in a relationship." Or "I am willing to risk loving and being loved," or "I learn from my past relationships and create even better ones in the future."

This exercise helps you to get into the "energy" of wanting something and then acting as if you have it now. Remember the story about my client who wanted to change her living space? When she was able to accept her current living space (it is what it is and it is home), she was also able to create the vision of where she wanted to be (act as if I already have it). This activated the ability for her vision or goal to become a reality. When you stay in the energy of want, that is where you will stay. If you create the energy of "have" through your vision, passion, effort and focus, you will have it.

This now concludes the portion of the book showing strategies to live your best life. The various exercises are designed to get you excited about setting goals for yourself to live your best life if you already are not doing so. I will summarize the exercises once more so you can set up your checklist of important and necessary "work" to get you connected and in the flow of all the good things in your life.

SUMMARY OF STRATEGIES

1. Heart-based breathing: connection to power centre, a.k.a. heart
2. Emotional releases: Heart wall and *The Emotion Code* book
3. Mindfulness practices
4. Daily practices: morning, evening, one-minute reboot, HeartMath – Global Coherence Initiative, journaling, pay attention, shadow work (emotional releases)
5. Vision, mission and values exercise: Stephen Covey example; six questions about yourself
6. Creating a vision, setting goals and creating belief statements for your life

Conclusion

The gift of life is a blessing. Each one of us was born "on purpose." When I think about the evolution of our planet, I can't help but think that we each have a gift, talent and passion that needs our attention and intention to manifest in this lifetime. There are no coincidences or accidents. The work to connect with our inner genius is an important and necessary step to living our best life. Now is the time to do the work.

> ***Each one of us was born "on purpose."***

I have always been intrigued by the mystery of life and the human experience. Many of my earlier passions and interests had me acting like a detective to uncover the data, information and knowledge that I have outlined in this book. I never connected that it was my purpose and gift to use these detective skills to discover a "possible" answer to this mystery called life.

It wasn't until the birth of my grandchildren that I realized that the impulse to write this book was actually going to become a reality. Through watching each one of them experience their new world for the first time, I was awakened to the truth that each one of us came into the world exactly the same way.

On a personal level, through the process of life happening, I experienced the disconnection from my heart and to the child-like wonder that allowed me to feel the joy of self-discovery and curiosity. It was my grandchildren that awakened the impulse to open my heart again. They taught me to find my joy. and because of them, this book is now a reality.

The direction my life has taken in the last 20 years has shifted my mindset and beliefs about life significantly. I now know that the only limitations on my dreams are the ones that I put on my "self." I am the one in charge of my life. I am empowered to design and create my experiences through consciousness and presence. I celebrate the "take a breath" moments as I get to rediscover the parts of me I left behind when I thought I was not "worthy" of a life that allowed me to be the star of my human experience. You just have to spend a few moments watching a child at play to know that they get it.

My vision for my grandchildren and future generations is that they are taught about their true nature so that they never forget or disconnect from the truth of who they are. Love is heart energy, and all the magic that exists here can be made real when we stay in the flow of life and all that it brings to us to experience.

My hope is that the seed of your potential grows in a field with all the right conditions to open up your world to every possibility that you can imagine. I have come to know that LOVE and LIGHT are the frequencies of healing. Those frequencies of energy connect us all to the conditions required to live to our potential and life purpose.

LOVE and LIGHT are the frequencies of healing.

The lyrics to Whitney Houston's song *The Greatest Love of All* sung in her self-titled album in 1985 became a "take a breath" moment for me. In 1986, shortly after the birth of my second daughter, this song touched me deeply, and I remember thinking how I wanted my daughters to be strong, independent and confident women who grew up knowing that they were the most important person in their own life and that they were loved. Now with three beautiful daughters, three amazing sons-in-law, five grandchildren and the sixth on the way, I want all of them to know this as a truth.

Here are the song's lyrics for you to take in and maybe even listen to Whitney sing as you read.

THE GREATEST LOVE OF ALL

Verse 1

I believe the children are our future
Teach them well and let them lead the way

Show them all the beauty they possess inside
Give them a sense of pride to make it easier
Let the children's laughter remind us how we used to be
Everybody's searching for a hero
People need someone to look up to
I never found anyone who fulfilled my needs
A lonely place to be
And so I learned to depend on me

Pre chorus:

I decided long ago
Never to walk in anyone's shadows
If I failed, if I succeed
At least I'll live as I believe
No matter what they take from me
They can't take away my dignity

Chorus

Because the greatest love of all
Is happening to me
I found the greatest love of all
Inside of me
The greatest love of all
Is easy to achieve
Learning to love yourself
It is the greatest love of all

The message to those of you who have connected to the content of this book is that you are the most important person in your life. Wake up to this truth and begin the journey "inward" to re-remember and rediscover all of the qualities that you possess to become a success in your life. Dream your most magnificent dreams and allow that vision to become your reality. Do the work, stay focused and present and know that you are worth it.

Living your best life is about discovering the joy and love in "you" and then expanding that "energy" outward so that you can attract more of into your life. YOU are the source and YOU are the only one that can control how you experience the next best part of your life.

YOU are the source and YOU are the only one that can control how you experience the next best part of your life.

Every journey always begins with the first step. This book was written with the intention of making the first and the next steps easier on the journey of connecting to your heart and to the life that you were meant to live. All you have to do is love yourself first and start from there.

The good news is the compass is pointing north, and YOU are the direction you are headed. So do the work, stay the course and may all your dreams become your reality. TAKE A BREATH and connect with the energy of your heart, and trust that you are not alone. Have faith and then surrender to the truth that YOU are the answer you have been SEEKING to live your best life.

Blessings to you, and may love and gratitude be the frequency of your heart, mind and spirit as you begin your journey home to YOU.

Acknowledgments

Without the guidance and support of the following people, this book would never have been possible.

Kristina Jansz: Life Skills and Empowerment Strategies. Kristina was my first spiritual coach/mentor and healer. She guided me to go inward and rediscover my "self." Her intuitive abilities are the most amazing gifts that she carries, and I was so blessed to have been guided by her at a time I needed it the most.

Pam and Allan Holt. Reflexology Teachers/Mentors/Healers. They saw me through my healing crisis with compassion and presence. The Holt School of Reflexology provided an excellent educational opportunity to understand energy and the capacity to use it for the greater good.

Victoria "Gentlebird" Wilde: Traditional Energy Healer/Clairvoyant Seer and Spiritual Guide. Victoria taught me so much through Sharing Circles, Native Teachings, Sacred Healing Journeys and so much more. She is a wonderful healer/teacher and guide.

Derek Rydall: Transformation Life Coach/Mentor/Teacher/Author. It was with Derek's personal guidance over a 10-month period and numerous programs he offered that I was able to learn, understand and apply the concepts of emergence and the journey to crack open the seed of potential within my "self." He is an amazing teacher and guide. His books and programs are top notch.

Dean Noblett and Rebecca Couch: Reiki Masters/Teachers; Heartlight. Dean and Rebecca are amazing teachers/mentor/guides and friends who open their hearts and home to teach Reiki and offer monthly gatherings during the full moon to celebrate oneness and the interconnectedness of all living beings. They have been a source of great comfort and support as I navigated through my understanding and connection to energy and the power of love.

Dr. Bradley Nelson: The Emotion Code/Body Code System. I was blessed to be part of Dr. Brad's first coaching program for EC/BC practitioners. It was an experience that provided me with the knowledge I needed to begin my own practice in energy and healing. I am grateful for his guidance and support.

To all of the other teachers and instructors I have worked with as I trained in Psych-K, Therapeutic Touch Levels 1–3, and Integrated Energy Therapy. It was in learning the nature of energy through different modalities that I gained a much broader perspective and capacity to develop specialized services for my clients. I am so grateful for the data and information that were made available for me to become the coach, mentor and teacher I am today.

The most important acknowledgement goes out to my family. To my husband, **Scott**, who was my greatest source of inspiration to get this book written. He inspires me daily through example, and I am proud to say after over 40 years of marriage that we continue to use the process of "take a breath" to navigate through our life together.

My three daughters, **Courtney, Lesley and Kelsey**, have been the source of my greatest love. Each one of them is a unique expression of life and we are so proud of them. They each carry amazing gifts of kindness, generosity and love. The three of them have found their life partners and have started families of their own. Our sons-in-law, **Shane, Marc and Carlo**, are amazing humans and have added so much more to our family with their presence and connection.

My grandchildren, to date**, Bryson, Liam, Taylor, Zoey and Willow**, are "perfect" in every way. Every moment I get to spend with them is like "a breath" of fresh air and new beginnings. The true nature of love shines through their eyes as they grow into their world. They teach me every day to "be me." I love them "to the moon and back."

To my sister, **Sandy**, thank you for all the words of encouragement and believing in my desire to write this book. To my brothers, **Bill and Paul**, may you enjoy the read and figure out a little bit more about me and how I think. Hope you smile and remember you were part of my journey to see the light.

To my mom, **Wilma**, who is now deceased, and my dad, **Jim**, at 93 years of age, thank you for the gift of life and the opportunity to survive and thrive in the circle of your unconditional love. I hope you are proud and know that you are loved and cherished for all that you have done and continue to do for our family.

To my extended family, which there are too many to mention, I wish you to know that we are connected because we were meant to be. We came to be with each other because there were lessons to learn and to teach. My hope is that we wake up to the messages and learn to stay present in the energy of our hearts as we move to the next best day of our life. Love to you all.

To my readers, thank you for picking up this book. I hope you enjoyed the content and found a "pearl" of wisdom among the pages to guide you forward on your journey. I send you love, light and blessings. My prayer is that your heart is open, and you feel the "energy" of love connecting you to all the possibilities that are waiting for you to discover as you live your best life.

Resources

The following list of books inspired and taught me what I have come to know and believe about energy, healing and the evolution of our soul's purpose. I offer them to you as a means to tap into the areas that interest you and to allow you to dig deeper into knowing your "self."

Altea, Rosemary. *The Eagle and the Rose: A Remarkable True Story*. New York: Grand Central Publishing, 1995.

Altea, Rosemary. *Give the Gift of Healing*. New York: Harper Collins,1997.

Altea, Rosemary. *Proud Spirit*. New York: Willliam Morrow Paperbacks, 1997.

Andrews, Ted. *Animal Speak*. Woodbury, Minnesota: Llewellyn Publishing, 2008.

Artnz, W., Chasse, B., and Vicente, M. *What the Bleep Do We Know*. Deerfield Beach, Florida: Health Communications, 2003.

Balsch, Phyllis A., and Balsch, James F. *Prescription for Dietary Wellness*. New York: Avery, 2003.

Balsch, Phyllis A., and Balsch, James F. *Prescription for Nutritional Healing*. New York: Penguin Putnam, 2000.

Bolte Taylor, Jill. *My Stroke of Insight*. New York: Viking, 2006.

Braden, Gregg. *The Isaiah Effect*. New York: Three Rivers Press, 2000.

Braden, Gregg. *The God Code*. Carlsbad, California: Hay House, 2004.

Braden, Gregg. *The Last Mode of Prayer*. Carlsbad, California: Hay House, 2006.

Braden, Gregg. *The Divine Matrix*. Carlsbad, California: Hay House, 2007.

Braden, Gregg. *Fractal Time*. Carlsbad, California: Hay House, 2009.

Braden, Gregg. *Spontaneous Healing of Belief*. Carlsbad, California: Hay House, 2009.

Braiker, Harriet B. *The Disease to Please.* New York: McGraw-Hill, 2001.

Brennan, Barbara Ann. *Hands of Light.* New York: Bantam Books, 1987.

Brennan, Barbara Ann. *Light Emerging.* New York: Bantam Books, 1993.

Brown, Brene. *The Gifts of Imperfection.* Danvers, Massachusetts: Hazelden, 2010.

Brown, Brene. *Daring Greatly.* New York: Avery, 2012.

Brown, Brene. *Rising Strong.* New York: Spiegel & Grau, 2015.

Buckingham, Marcus, and Clifton, Donald O. *Now, Discover your Strengths.* New York: The Free Press, 2001.

Burnham, Sophy. *The Art of Intuition.* Toronto, Ontario: Penguin, 2014.

Byrne, Lorna. *Love from Heaven.* New York: Atria Books, 2014.

Cayce, Edgar. *The Sleeping Prophet.* New York: Doubleday,1967.

Chapman, Gary. *The 5 Love Languages.* Chicago, Illinois: Northfield Publishing, 2015.

Chopra, Deepak. *Quantum Healing.* New York: Bantam Books,1989.

Chopra, Deepak. *Ageless Body, Timeless Mind.* New York: Harmony Books, 1993.

Chopra, Deepak. *How to Know God.* New York: Harmony Books, 2000.

Chopra, Deepak. *Buddha.* San Francisco, California: Harper One, 2007.

Chopra, Deepak. *Why Is God Laughing.* New York: Harmony Books, 2008.

Chopra, Deepak. *Reinventing the Body, Resurrecting the Soul.* New York: Harmony Books, 2009.

Collier, Robert. *The Secret of the Ages.* Toronto, Ontario: Penguin Books, 2007.

Cota-Robles, Patricia Diane. *Take Charge of Your Life.* Tucson, Arizona: New Age Study of Humanities Purpose,1996.

Cota-Robles, Patricia Diane. *The Next Step.* Tucson, Arizona: New Age Study of Humanities Purpose,1994.

Cota-Robles, Patricia Diane. *The Awakening: Eternal Youth, Vibrant Health, Radiant Beauty.* Tucson, Arizona: New Age Study of Humanities Purpose, 1993.

Cota-Robles, Patricia Diane. *Stargate of the Heart.* Tucson, Arizona: New Age Study of Humanities Purpose, 1994.

Cota-Robles, Patricia Diane. *What on Earth Is Going On.* Tucson, Arizona: New Age Study of Humanities Purpose, 1997.

Cota-Robles, Patricia Diane. *Who Am I? Why Am I Here.* Tucson, Arizona: New Age Study of Humanities Purpose, 1997.

Cota-Robles, Patricia Diane. *Home: Heaven on Mother Earth.* Tucson, Arizona: New Age Study of Humanities Purpose, 2003.

Cota-Robles, Patricia Diane. *The Violet Flame.* Tucson, Arizona: New Age Study of Humanities Purpose, 2007.

Cota-Robles, Patricia Diane. *I Am Co-creating the New Earth: A Book of Invocation.* Tucson, Arizona: New Age Study of Humanities Purpose, 2008.

Covey, Stephen. *7 Habits of Highly Effective People.* New York: Simon & Schuster,1989.

Covey, Stephen. *First Things First.* New York: *Simon & Schuster, 1994.*

Davidson, Richard J., and Begley, Sharon. *The Emotional Life of Your Brain.* New Yor: Hudson Street Pres, 2012.

Dispenza, Joe. *The Science of Changing Your Mind.* Taylor & Francis Deerfield Beach, Florida: Health Communications, 2007.

Doidge, Norman. *The Brain's Way of Healing.* New York: Viking, 2015.

Eade, Betty. *Embraced by the Light.* New York: Bantam Books/Gold Leaf Press, 1992.

Eden, Donna. *Energy Medicine.* Toronto, Ontario: Penguin, 2008.

Eden, Donna. *Energy Medicine for Woman.* Toronto, Ontario: Penguin, 2008.

Eich, Thomas, *The Work of Bruno Gruening.* Monchengladbach, Germany: Grete Hausler CmbH Vertag, 2003.

Emoto, Masara. *The True Power of Water.* New York: Atria Books/ Beyond Words, 2003.

Farmer, Steven D. *Animal Spirit Guides.* Carlsbad, California: Hay House, 2006.

Foundation for Inner Peace. *A Course in Miracles.* New York: Viking/Penguin Group, 1996.

Gach, Michael Reed, and Henning, Beth Ann. *Acupressure for Emotional Healing.* New York: Bantam Books, 2004.

Gawain, Shakti. *Creative Visualization.* Weymouth, Massachusetts: New World Library/Nataraj Publishing, 1978.

Gilbert, Elizabeth. *Eat, Pray, Love.* Toronto, Ontario: Penguin, 2006.

Gilbert, Elizabeth. *Big Magic.* Toronto, Ontario: Penguin, 2015.

Gladwell, Malcolm. *Outliers.* New York: Little, Brown Co., 2008.

Goldsmith, Joel S. *The Art of Spiritual Healing.* San Francsico, California: Harper One,1992.

Goldsmith, Joel S. *The Art of Meditation.* San Francsico, California: Harper One, 1990.

Goldsmith, Joel S. *Practicing Presence.* San Francsico, California: Harper One, 1991.

Goldsmith, Joel S. *Living the Infinite Way.* Atlanta, Georgia: Acropolis Books, 2013.

Gordon, Richard. *Quantum Touch: The Power to Heal.* Berkley, California: North Atlantic Books,2006.

Green, Glenda. *Love without End.* Toronto, ON: Spiritus Publishing, 2009.

Green, Glenda. *The Keys of Jeshua.* Toronto, ON: Spiritus Publishing, 2007.

Hawkes, Joyce Whiteley. *Cell-Level Healin:, The Bridge from Soul to Cell.* New York: Atria Books/Beyond Words, 2006.

Hawkins, David R. *Power vs. Force.* Carlsbad, California: Hay House, 2002.

Hay, Louise L. *You Can Heal Your Life.* Carlsbad, California: Hay House, 1999.

Hay, Louise L. *Meditations to Heal Your Life.* Carlsbad, California: Hay House, 2002.

Hay, Louise L. *You Can Heal Your Life Companion Book.* Carlsbad, California: Hay House, 2002.

Hocking, Bruce. *Natural Health I: ETPS Neuro Mechanical Acupuncture.* Etobicoke, ON: Acumed Medical Publishing *1996.*

Hocking, Bruce. *Natural Health: ETPS Neuro Mechanical Acupuncture Manual.* Etobicoke, On: Acumed Medical Publishing.1998.

Hubbard, Barbara Marx. *Emergence.* Newburyport, Massachusetts: Hampton Roads, 2001.

Hubbard, Barbara Marx. *52 Codes for Conscious Self Evolution.* http://theawakenedpress.com: Awakened World Press, 2011.

Hubbard, Barbara Marx. *Birth 2012.* Newburyport, Mass.: Red Wheel/Weiser, 2012.

Judith, Amodea. *Eastern Body, Western Mind.* Celestial Arts,1996.

Judith, Amodea. *Wheels of Life.* Woodbury, Minnesota: Llewellyn Publications, 2002.

Kingma, Daphne Rose. *The Future of Love.* New York: Doubleday, 1998.

Kinkade, Amelia. *Straight from the Horse's Mouth.* Novato, California: New World Library, 2001.

Kinkade, Amelia. *The Language of Miracles.* Novato, California: New World Library, 2006.

Kubler-Ross, Elizabeth. *On Death and Dying.* New York: Scribner, 1969.

Kubler-Ross, Elizabeth. *On Life after Death.* Berkeley, California: Celestial Arts, 2008.

Kubler-Ross, Elizabeth, and Kessler, David. *On Grief and Grieving.* New York: Scribner, 2005.

Laporte, Danielle. *The Desire Map: A Guide to Creating Goals with Soul.* Louisville, Colorado: Sounds True, 2014.

Lerma, John. *Into the Light.* Newburyport, Massachusetts: Career Press, 2007.

Lerma, John. *Learning from the Light.* Newburyport, Massachusetts: Career Press, 2009.

Lian, Yu-Lin, Chen, Chun Yang, Hammes, Michael, and Kolster, Bernard C. *Pictorial Atlas of Acupuncture.* Potsdam, Germany: H.F. Ullmann Publishing, 2005.

Lincoln, Michael J. *Messages from the Body: Their Psychological Meaning.* Spring Creek, Nevada: Talking Hearts, 2006.

Lipton, Bruce. *The Biology of Belief.* Carlsbad, California: Hay House, 2005

Lipton, Bruce. *The Honeymoon Effect.* Carlsbad, California: Hay House, 2013.

Lipton, Bruce, and Bhaerman, Steve. *Spontaneous Evolution.* Carlsbad, California: Hay House, 2009.

Loyd, Alexander. *The Healing Codes.* New York: Grand Central Life and Style, 2010.

Marieb. Elaine N. *Anatomy and Physiology Coloring Book.* New York: Daryl Fox, 2000.

Marieb. Elaine N. *Essentials of Human Anatomy and Physiology.* San Francisco, California: Benjamin Cummings, 2003.

Mate, Gabor. *When the Body Says No.* Toronto, Ontario: Vintage Canada, 2004.

May, Diane. *The Therapeutic Touch Handbooks, Levels 1–3.* Pontiac, Michigan: Scribe Press,2003.

McTaggert, Lynne. *The Intention Experiment.* New York: Free Press, 2007.

McTaggert, Lynne. *The Field.* New York: Harper, 2008.

McTaggert, Lynne. *The Bond.* New York: Free Press, 2011.

McTaggert, Lynne. *The Power of 8.* New York: Atria Books, 2017.

Mear, Lloyd, and Mear, Phyllis. *Energy Balancing by Numbers.* Balancingbynumbers.com: Christine Danyi, 2014.

Megre, Vladimer. *Anastasia Series Books 1–8.* ringingcedarsofrussia.org: Ringing Cedars Press,2006.

Mehl-Madrona, Lewis. *Coyote Medicine.* New York: Simon & Schuster, 1998.

Mercola, Joseph. *Effortless Healing.* New York: Harmony, 2015.

Merry, Peter. *Evolutionary Leadership.* London, Ontario: Integral Publishing, 2009.

Myss, Caroline. *Anatomy of the Spirit.* New York: Three Rivers Press, 1996.

Myss, Caroline. *Why People Don't Heal and How They Can.* New York: Three Rivers Press,1997.

Myss, Caroline. *Sacred Contracts.* New York: Harmony, 2003.

Myss, Caroline. *Invisible Acts of Power.* New York: Free Press, 2004.

Nelson, Bradley. *The Emotion Code.* Mesquite, Nevada: Wellness Unmasked Publishers, 2007.

Nelson, Kevin. *Spiritual Doorway in the Brain.* Boston, Massachusetts: Dutton, 2011.

Ober, Clinton, Sinatra, Stephen, and Zucker, Martin. *Earthing.* Columbus, Ohio: Basic Health Publications, 2010.

Papastavro, Tellis S. *The Gnosis and the Law.* Tucson, Arizona: New Age of Humanity's Purpose, 1972.

Pearl, Eric. *The Reconnection: Heal Others, Heal Yourself.* Carlsbad, California: Hay House, 2001.

Pearsall, Paul. *The Heart's Code.* New York: Broadway Books, 1998.

Pert, Candace B. *Molecules of Emotion.* New York: Scribner,1997.

Pinel, John P., and Edwards, Maggie. *A Colourful Introduction to the Anatomy of the Brain.* Boston, Massachusetts: Allyn and Bacon,1998.

Randa, Therese H. *How to Go on Living when Someone You Love Dies.* Washington, DC: Lexington Books,1988.

Riso, Richard Don, and Hudson, Russ. *The Wisdom of the Enneagram.* New York: Bantam Books, 1999.

Rock, David. *Your Brain at Work.* New York: Harper Business, 2009.

Ruiz, Don Miguel. *The Four Agreements.* San Rafael, California: Amber-Allen Publishing, 1997.

Ruiz, Don Miguel. *The Mastery of Love.* San Rafael, California: Amber-Allen, 1999.

Ruiz, Don Miguel. *The Four Agreements Companion Book.* San Rafael, California: Amber-Allen Publishing, 2000.

Ruiz, Don Miguel. *The Voice of Knowledge.* San Rafael, California: Amber-Allen Publishing, 2004.

Ruiz, Don Miguel. *The Fifth Agreement.* San Rafael, California: Amber-Allen Publishing, 2010.

Ruiz, Don Miguel. *Living a Life of Awareness.* San Antonio, Texas: Hierophant Publishing, 2013.

Ruiz, Don Miguel. *The 5 Levels of Attachment.* San Antonio, Texas: Hierophant Publishing, 2013.

Ruiz, Don Miguel. *The Toltec Art of Life and Death.* New York: Harper Elixir, 2015.

Rydall, Derek. *Emergence.* New York: Atria Books, 2015.

Rydall, Derek. *The Abundance Project.* New York: Atria Books, 2018.

Seale, Alan. *The Manifestation Wheel.* San Francisco, California: Weiser Books, 2008.

Siegel, Bernie. *The Mindfulness Solution.* New York: Guilford Press, 2010.

Siegel, Ronald. *Love, Medicine and Miracles.* New York: William Morrow, 2002.

Singer, Michael J. *The Untethered Soul.* Oakland, California: New Harbinger Publication, 2007.

Tappe, Nancy A. *Understanding Your Life through Colour.* Addison, Texas: Aquila Libris Publishing, 2009.

Tappe, Nancy A., and Altaris, Kathy. *Indigos: The Quiet Storm.* Addison, Texas: Aquila Media Productions, 2011.

Thayer, Steven. *The Healing Angels of the Energy Field.* New York: The Center of Being Inc., 2001.

Thich Nhat Hanh. *The Energy of Prayer: How to Deepen Your Spiritual Practice.* Berkeley, California: Parallax Press, 2006.

Thich Nhat Hanh. *Fear.* San Francisco, California: Harper One, 2012.

Tipping, Colin. *Radical Forgiveness.* Los Angeles, California: Global 13 Productions, 2002.

Tipping, Colin. *Spiritual Intelligence of Work.* Los Angeles, California: Global 13 Productions, 2004.

Tolle, Eckhart. *The Power of Now.* Vancouver, British Columbia: Namaste Publishing,1997.

Tolle, Eckhart. *Practicing the Power of Now.* Novato, California: New World Library, 1999.

Tolle, Eckhart. *A New Earth.* New York: Dutton, 2005.

Villoldo, Alberto. *Shaman, Healer, Sage.* New York: Harmony Books, 2000.

Villoldo, Alberto. *Courageous Dreaming.* Carlsbad, California: Hay House, 2008.

Villoldo, Alberto. *The Illumination Process.* Carlsbad, California: Hay House, 2017.

Villoldo, Alberto. *The Heart of a Shaman.* Carlsbad, California: Hay House, 2018.

Villoldo, Alberto. *Grow a New Body.* Carlsbad, California: Hay House, 2019

Villoldo, Alberto, and Perlmuter, David. *Power Up Your Brain: The Neuroscience of Enlightenment.* Carlsbad, California: Hay House, 2011.

Walsch, Neale Donald. *Conversations with God, Books 1–3.* Newburyport, Massachusetts: Hampton Road, 1995–1998.

Walsch, Neale Donald. *Friendship with God.* New York: Putnam, 1999.

Walsch, Neale Donald. *Communion with God.* New York: Putnam, 2000.

Walsch, Neale Donald. *The New Revelations.* New York: Atria Books, 2002.

Walsch, Neale Donald. *Tomorrow's God.* New York: Atria Books, 2004.

Walsch, Neale Donald. *Home with God.* New York: Atria Books, 2006.

Walsch, Neale Donald. *Happier than God.* Newburyport, Massachusetts: Hampton Roads, 2008.

Walsch, Neale Donald. *When Everything Changes Change Everything.* New York: EmNim Book, 2009.

Weiss, Brian. *Messages from the Masters.* New York: Grand Central Publishing, 2000.

Wilber, Pallen. *A Brief History of Everything.* Boulder, Colorado: Shambhala, 2000.

Wilber, Pallen. *Integral Psychology.* Boulder, Colorado: Shambhala, 2000.

Wilber, Pallen, and Leonard, Morellie. *Integral Life Practices.* London, Ontario: Integral Books, 2008.

Wilde, Stuart. *Miracles.* Carlsbad, California: Hay House, 1988.

Wilde, Stuart. *The Infinite Self.* Carlsbad, California: Hay House, 1996.

Wilde, Stuart. *Sixth Sense.* Carlsbad, California: Hay House, 2000.

Wilde, Stuart. *The Art of Redemption.* Carlsbad, California: Hay House, 2007.

Wilde, Stuart. *Grace, Gaia and the End Days.* Carlsbad, California: Hay House, 2009.

William, Anthony. *Medical Medium.* Carlsbad, California: Hay House, 2015.

Williams, Robert M. *Psych-K: The Missing Peace in Your Life.* www.myrddnpublishing.com: Myrddin Publications, 2008.

Williamson, Marianne. *A Return to Love.* New York: Harper Perennial, 1992.

Williamson, Marianne. *A Woman's Worth.* New York: Random House, 1993.

Williamson, Marianne. *The Healing of America.* New York: Simon & Schuster, 1997.

Williamson, Marianne. *Everyday Grace.* New York: Riverhead Books, 2002.

Williamson, Marianne. *The Gift of Change.* San Francisco, California: Harper, 2004.

Williamson, Marianne. *The Age of Miracles.* Carlsbad, California: Hay House, 2008.

Williamson, Marianne. *The Law of Divine Compensation.* San Francisco, California: Harper One, 2012.

Williamson, Marianne. *A Year of Miracles.* San Francisco, California: Harper One, 2013.

Wills, Pauline. *Colour Reflexology for Health and Healing.* Detroit, Michigan: Vega, 2002.

CPSIA information can be obtained
at www.ICGtesting.com
Printed in the USA
LVHW082007270520
656172LV00007BA/34/J

9 780228 827580